D1548044

Between Crisis and Catastrophe

BETWEEN CRISIS AND CATASTROPHE

Lyrical and Mystical Essays

by

ANDREI BELY

Compiled and Translated
by

BORIS JAKIM

First published in the USA
by Semantron Press
Translation & Introduction

Semantron Press is an imprint of
Angelico Press

For information, address:
Angelico Press, Ltd.
4709 Briar Knoll Dr. Kettering, OH 45429
www.angelicopress.com

Paperback: 978-1-62138-172-3
eBook: 978-1-62138-173-0

Cover design: Michael Schrauzer

CONTENTS

Translator's Introduction

1

Andrei Bely (1880–1934) was the greatest Russian writer of the 20th century. Chiefly known outside of Russia as a novelist (his *Petersburg* is the greatest 20th-century Russian novel, often compared to Joyce's *Ulysses*), he was also a leading symbolist poet and a profound philosophical critic. Bely was also a mystic who had an unsurpassed ability to express his visions in writing, and he often did so in the form of lyrical essays, a selection of which is offered here.

Many of the essays in this volume were written as the new century began, and they express a sense of apocalypse, a sense that humanity was on the threshold of a new epoch. For Bely a new religious consciousness was emerging, rooted in Solovyov's visions of Sophia and Nietzsche's proclamation that a new man was on the verge of being created. A new dawn—both joyful and terrifying—was already visible on the horizon.

2

In "Window into the Future," "The Phoenix," "The Mask," and "The Song of Life" we find a lyricism approaching music: "A solitary nebula is condensing, preparing at some point to give birth to suns, to eject a myriad of flaming jewels—red rubies and cosmic amethysts—onto the shore of time. . . . The known will be overwhelmed by the unknown, and this city with houses, palaces, and temples will fly apart like an ancient phantom that has more than once troubled the quietude of Eternity."[1] Our problem is that "we have forgotten how to fly. We think heavily and walk heavily; the heroic is lost to us and our life-rhythm is

1. See "Windows into the Future," p. 5.

attenuated."[2] There is only one solution: to regain lightness, divine simplicity, and health. Only then "will we be able to sing boldly our life, for if living life is not song, then life is not life."[3]

In "Sacred Colors," we expect to find a religious interpretation of colors, but what we actually get is a mystical meditation on the future of humanity: "The finality of Christianity, the New Testament nature of the thought of the end, the unexpected lightness and joy which are invariably contained in this thought—this is the light that has descended into our soul. Where does this come from? And why? When the dust scatters and the air's whiteness begins to glisten, suddenly we will see the heavenly blue. And in the bright white of the day we will learn to recognize our joy by gazing at the sorrowfully joyful clear azure sky."[4] Our joy and our life come from the sky, and "when the dust scatters," eternal joy and life will descend into our souls like the shining of the sun.

In "Tolstoy" and "Recollections of Vladimir Solovyov" we get reflections on two of Bely's great contemporaries, both of whom he knew personally. For Bely, Tolstoy showed the Russian people an ideal of holiness: "he built a bridge to the people: religion and areligiosity, silence and words, the creativity of life and artistic creativity, the intelligentsia and the people—all these things merged in the final eloquent gesture of genius of the dying Tolstoy."[5]

Bely's memoir of Solovyov is unique and irreplaceable. Particularly memorable is his description of Solovyov, shortly before his death, reading from the "Tale about the Antichrist": "when he arrived at the words 'Elder John rose like a white candle,' he rose up from his armchair. Lightning was flashing in the window and Solovyov's face was trembling in a lightning of inspiration."[6] Here, Solovyov himself, transfigured, enters into the realm of the Apocalypse, becoming one of its figures, comparable to the "Woman clothed in the sun."

2. See "Song of Life," p. 49.
3. Ibid.
4. See "Sacred Colors," p. 65.
5. See "Tolstoy," p. 74.
6. See "Recollections of Vladimir Solovyov," p. 84.

In "Apocalypse in Russian Poetry" Bely emerges as a full-fledged follower of Solovyov, the sophianic poet who had three personal meetings with the "Woman clothed in the sun." Bely sees Russian poetry evolving toward an apocalypse in which this poetry will be transformed into living life. "The problem raised by this poetry can be solved only by the transformation of Earth and Heaven into the city of New Jerusalem. The apocalypse of Russian poetry is brought about by the approach of the end of universal history."[7]

There is nothing comparable in world literature to Bely's essay "The Crisis of Culture." Weaving together reflections on Nietzsche and St. Augustine, ruminations on Schubert's song cycles, and his own profound mystical experiences, in particular his joys and tribulations as an anthroposophist,[8] Bely proclaims the end of the old epoch of decrepitude and the beginning of a new epoch of spiritual awakening. He shares with us his own remarkable inner experiences: "I'd sit down in a comfortable armchair on the little terrace hanging over the pines, the strata of stones, and the fjord; and I'd concentrate all my attention on the thoughts that were sucking into themselves my feelings and impulses. My body, covered with rhythms of thought, did not hear the inertia of its organs; some clear thing within me was flying through my skull into vastnesses; it zestfully propelled itself by rhythms as if by wings. . . . I was multi-winged; sparks were shooting out of my eyes and weaving themselves together; the weaving of the sparks created images for me: a crucified dove woven of light, headless wings, and a winged crystal, twisting themselves into spirals. . . . Once I saw a sign: a triangle composed of lightnings, placed on an ultra-luminous crystal and emitting cosmoses of light; and within it there was an 'eye'. . . ."[9]

7. See "Apocalypse in Russian Poetry," p. 103.

8. In 1913 Bely became an adherent of Rudolf Steiner and joined his anthroposophical colony in Basel, Switzerland. For a number of years Bely was an active member of the anthroposophical movement, participating among other things in the construction of the Johannes Building in Dornach. He later broke with the Steiner group.

9. See "Crisis of Culture," p. 142. The translation given here is slightly different from that given on p. 142.

3

Bely's language in this volume is full of cosmic, meteorological, and other natural images: whirlwinds, clouds, simooms, blizzards, sunsets and crimson dawns, haze, swirls of dust, river currents, nebulae, cosmic abysses. And everything is dominated by the sophianic image of the "Woman clothed in the sun." These images seem apt since Bely is talking about the destruction of the old world and the birth of a new one. Here are two examples: "The whirlwind that is blowing in our Russia, swirling up all the dust, must inevitably create the specter of a red terror, a cloud of smoke and fire, since light sets dust afire when it suffuses it."[10] "The Norwegian sunset, engulfing the surroundings, amazes me. A serene clarity transubstantiates the fjords; the movement of the air stretches the distances; a bright-pawed cloud hangs suspended; lemon-colored bands of moisture pour down, turn into mist, and disappear."[11]

The notes are the translator's except where indicated otherwise.

BORIS JAKIM
January 1, 2016

10. See "Apocalypse in Russian Poetry," p. 90.
11. See "Crisis of Culture," p. 140.

Window into the Future[1]

The Whirl

Millions of centuries fly in space and wash away the sun, and wash away one another, like transitory waves.

Here world has fallen onto world. Planets that had cooled have caught fire again.

Over there, a solitary nebula is condensing, preparing at some point to give birth to suns and to eject a myriad of flaming jewels onto the shore of time. Nations will war against nations amidst unchanging spaces on cold crusts of fire erupting from the maws of countless volcanoes.

Then everything will settle down. The known will be overwhelmed by the unknown, and this city with houses, palaces, and temples will fly apart like an ancient phantom that has more than once troubled the quietude of Eternity.

It is the unknown that has caused the nebulae to condense. Chinese sages call it "Tao." "Tao" shakes the etheric folds of worlds. Out of the etheric folds will sprinkle, like the scattered splashes of rockets, millions of sparkling images.

"Tao" glimmers eternally. It flies like a pale pearl in the azure satin; or it leaps off the mountain peaks and splashes like rain on the granites below. We say then that we see an idea.

We are beings who have emerged on the cold crust of fiery delirium. We have woven a radiant essence into a spiderweb fabric of concepts. And when "Tao" gazes at us, spreading apart the web, we say that madness is coming.

But are we not madmen when we repose in solitude in the ancient unknown and everything that is near is dispersed, like a nebula, in the cosmic?

1. First published in the magazine *Vesy*, 1904, no. 12.

Do we not then find strange that the apertures into the vastness are called "windows" and that the glistening flame is called a "lamp"?

The Symbol

A ray of light can penetrate a series of transparent glass-plates. It cannot spread reality over them. By covering it with an amalgam the glass must be transformed into a mirror. Only then will the immensity of the world be inversely captured in the mirroring surface.

That is what knowledge must be like, for the glass is a concept while the mirror is the concept raised to an idea.

Every thing has its shadow. The shadow of an idea is a concept. But a concept is not an idea.

An idea can touch a concept at a single point the way a tangent touches a circle. This possibility of fleeting contact is an endless source of errors, for idea is confused with concept. The task of the logical process of thought is to raise the investigated concept to an idea by moving it (as it were) along a circle to the place where the straight line touches this circle. The data of external experience will coincide then with internal data. You will gaze with astonishment where just recently you had understood.

In the uniformly illuminated surface of thought a breach is formed through which a bundle of light waves is emitted.

In art we gain knowledge of ideas by raising an image to a symbol. Symbolism is a method for the representation of ideas in images. Art cannot separate itself from symbolism, which can be either masked (as in classical art) or explicit (as in romanticism and neo-romanticism). Art always has a unifying element. Here a moment is taken when the folds of the cosmic spiderweb are spread apart: *that which had been external stops appearing so.* Comparison of an object or its parts with another object raises this object to *some third thing.* This *third thing* becomes a relation uniting the many into one, i.e., it becomes a symbol. And insofar as this relation compares the relative (phenomenal) features of objects, to that extent it reveals the relativity of the relative, directing by this method from the contrary the inner gaze to that which emerges from beneath the mask of relativity once this mask is disclosed. That is why in symbolism every complexification of relations will more fully disclose the inner which emerges from beneath the complexity. That is why the means of representation (comparison, metaphor, metonymy, etc.) are instruments of symbolism. The symbol is the shell of the idea, the shell of "Tao."

If the concept can be raised to the idea and the image can be raised to the symbol and if the symbol is always the shell of the idea, then symbolism conjoins the peaks of knowledge and intuition. It is the principle of a method uniting knowledge and creativity. It is revealed here that the data of different methods are projections of *the same thing* on different planes of being. We find that it is possible to seek the esoteric meaning of different externally sketched truths. From van der Waals' formula we can see what makes clouds coalesce in the azure and what threads them into a single necklace, stretching them along the horizon.

If a symbol is known from the relation of two phenomena touching at one point, then the relation of the essence (music) to its manifestation gives birth to a special class of symbols—tragic ones. The character of the relation of idea to appearance determines our understanding of the world: either the difference between images is abolished, disappearing into the depths; or the depths themselves, becoming embodied in this difference, impart increasingly greater distinctness to the images. Here we find the root of an inevitable duality in the relation to tragic myth. Nietzsche writes: "When we viewed the drama, our clairvoyant gaze penetrated into the inner world agitated by its motifs; and it seemed that a symbolic picture was unfurling before us. The absolute clarity of the picture did not satisfy us, for it seemed that it was simultaneously concealing and revealing something."[2] The tragic mask gazing at us with the smile of the Medusa is a source of puzzlement to us: What is gazing at us from behind the mask? Is it not the void staring at us? What are we to do if we rip off the mask and see that nobody is concealed behind it? What power is contained in the fateful smile of the Gorgon's head attached to the shield of Perseus who is as yet unknown to us, if even this mask is sometimes capable of transforming us into horrified stone statues? But this horror is an illusion. Is the radi-

2. From *The Birth of Tragedy.*

ance that unexpectedly shines upon us from behind the foggy folds of life not capable of blinding us? Perhaps in the very next instant its rays will destroy the enormous black spot that has illusorily grown between us and the light. The white countenance will turn toward us; the armor of Perseus, this new Apollo revealed to us, will flash out at us like lightning. "Wherever Dionysian waves heave turbulently, Apollo, concealed in a cloud, must also descend."[3]

The serpentine hair surrounds the Gorgon's mask like a dark cloud, but will it not sometimes be pierced by the radiance of divinity? Yes, the cloud has dissipated. It is no more.

Serpentine bands of little gray clouds fly by, revealing the shining of the divine armor.

Mystery

Nietzsche was the first to explore the relation between the Dionysian and Apollonian principles in all its universal historical meaning.

The mystery provided the form for the musical drama. The abysses revealed by the mystery were later covered over by the spiderweb fabric of Alexandrian eclecticism. Now we see that music has once again splashed out at us from behind this fabric. Therefore, is the mystery not the final link of the evolution we are experiencing? If it is, if drama is being transformed into mystery, the actor must become a priest and the spectator a participant in sacramental rites. Drama is being transformed into life so that sacred symbols can be forged from it. At the moment of tragic action we were compelled to gaze behind myth, as it were, in order to perceive its sacred, transfigurative meaning; and the thing that compelled us was the good news of a new day in which the tragic mask will fly off the face of the long-expected deity, come into the world. Nietzsche, who constantly underscores the consequences that follow from his thought, is as silent as the grave here. He understood too well the danger associated with calling the final conclusion of our culture a mystery. Such a conclusion would have compelled him to

3. Ibid.

speak of religion, and to speak of it in an absolutely new way, which perhaps would have been lethal to him personally.

That is why he sought salvation in music, calling the musical drama the final link that completes culture. That is why he was in haste to conjoin the converging lines of poetry and music by means of the name Wagner, while ignoring the fact that Wagner was only one of the pioneers who proclaimed the fusion of poetry and music—a fusion inevitably leading to mystery. In the further approach to the central transition point of our culture, Wagner with his *Parsifal* clarified for us the nature of this transition. He spoke (ineptly, to be sure) where Nietzsche would have bitten off his tongue; it's clear that Nietzsche regarded him as a traitor. It's at this point that Nietzsche made his fateful leap from Wagner to Bizet and from Schopenhauer to positivism. This leap had a profound effect on all of Nietzsche's further activity, introducing chaos and skepticism where the sun is still unable to shine.

If Nietzsche had looked into the eyes of the approaching future, he would not have expected anything truly tragic from Wagner's operas. Tragedy that descends to the depths of mystery is inevitably connected with simplicity. In antiquity people would gather to pray before the statue of a god. But there is no true prayer at the present time. If the essence of mystery is religious, it will appear neither in opera nor in drama.

Olenina-d'Alheim[4]

When this interpreter of spiritual depths stands before us, when she sings her songs to us, we do not dare say that her voice is not beyond reproach, that it is not a large voice.

We forget about the quality of her voice because she is more than just a singer.

The relation of music to poetic symbols deepens these symbols. Olenina-d'Alheim interprets these deepened symbols with a remarkable expressiveness. She shows her attitude toward the interpreted symbols

4. Maria Olenina-d'Alheim was a famous concert singer at the beginning of the 20th century who specialized in the songs of Mussorgsky.

by an inimitable play of her face. The poetic symbol—made complex by the relation of music to it, transformed by voice, and shaded by mimicry—expands immeasurably. The idea vividly emerges from the expanded and deepened symbol. Finally, a skillful selection of symbols makes it possible to express the idea more simply.

That is why, striking such a complex chord in the strings of our soul, she crosses the boundary between music and poetry. Outside of drama and opera, we cannot imagine an art that more fully unites poetry and music. But because of the complexity of the means necessary to perform them, drama and opera weaken the immediacy of the stream gushing out of Eternity. Contemporary drama and opera threaten to collapse under the ever-growing complexity of stagecraft. That is why the spiritual potential revealed in drama and opera must become something simple which abolishes both of them so that it can rise to greater heights. What is the best form for the mystery that is being born before us if not the fiery form of prophecies in song?

The absolute fusion of music and poetry is possible only in man's soul. That is why the union of music and poetry is capable of giving birth not to works of art but to personalities strong in spirit. These personalities must become the prototypes of a future priesthood.

That is why the appearance of such figures as Vladimir Solovyov, Nikisch,[5] and Olenina-d'Alheim is of great significance for our culture. The epoch of geniuses and great thinkers has passed. Here and there they are being replaced by personalities in whom we see a prophetic pathos and who are destined to unite life with mystery.

Olenina-d'Alheim unfurls before us the depths of spirit. On how she unfurls these depths and what she reveals before us lies the shadow of prophecy. That is why we strongly feel that she herself is a link uniting us with mystery.

Our consciousness is a fine boundary between the subconscious and the superconscious. Different relations between given psychic spheres cause variations in this boundary. By introducing new combinations of emotions into our soul through symbols that are being unfolded, we provide new material for our nerves. And since the variable atmosphere of nerve effects can lead to new regroupings of the material of

5. Arthur Nikisch (1855–1922), famous conductor.

our conscious activity, this atmosphere is capable of affecting variations of the boundary between the superconscious and the subconscious. The mysticism pouring out of the ancient songs in Olenina-d'Alheim's interpretation may turn out to be the lever with which we will overturn all of reality. By changing our psychic structure we will be able to change not only particular elements of consciousness but also the general forms of the latter.

Defined externally, religion is a system of successively unfolded symbols. This inner connectedness of symbols differentiates religious revelation from artistic creation. From the external side there is no boundary between art and religion. There is only a difference in the quality and quantity of internally connected images. The purpose of art is to express ideas; the deepening and purification of every idea invariably extend this idea to a universal significance. Thus, all idea-ness in art has a religious nuance.

The symbol that is deepened and expanded analogously to an idea is therefore connected with the universal symbol. This is the final and invariable background of all symbols. The relation of the Logos to the world Soul as the mystical principle of humanity is such a symbol. That is why the foundations of symbolism are always religious. That is why the complexity of the idea-symbols evoked by the singing of Olenina-d'Alheim makes her a servant of religion.

The Concert

With mask tied firmly to face, someone's negligently carefree black profile glides through electrically lighted halls. Above the abyss glide fashionable ladies, gazing through their lorgnettes and waving their fans. Above the abyss wave the tails of men's suits, with all buttons buttoned. All without exception are plugging up with their masks the yawning depths of their souls to keep away the cold drafts coming from the abysses of the spirit. When the winds of Eternity blow, these people are afraid of catching the cosmic fever.

Someone whispers to someone: "I hear she's a talented singer." And is that all there is?

No, no, of course "that's not all." But don't ask about anything; don't rip the veils off the soul when nobody knows what to do with the depths that have crept up. Everything is too unexpected. Can a dwarf act like a titan? Great feelings are horrifying when they appear without great deeds. Strange she is on the concert stage, strange because, having opened the sleepers' eyes, she abandons them instead of leading them to the sun. Let them hop up, those two gentlemen who are hiding their souls; let them snap their fingers on the poster. Now they incline their faces toward each other, like two conspirators, to exchange some banality. After all, these are not two surfaces approaching each other, but two depths covered with masks.

But quiet now, quiet.

A tall woman in black enters onto the stage in a somewhat awkward manner. There is something oppressive about her silhouette, something too large for a human being. It would be more appropriate to listen to her amidst abysses, to see her in the breaks of clouds. The sharp features of her face combine simplicity with extreme uncommonness. She is somehow overly simplified, overly strange. Her indefinite eyes burn us with an immense brightness, as if she has come close to stars through the flights of a misty life.

She sings.

Of that which we have forgotten but which has never forgotten us—of the dawn of golden happiness. And there will be no limit to that dawn, because there will be no limit to that happiness. It will be infinite. Her moans are like the wailing of a blizzard about how brother has killed brother. Out of distant cosmic spaces resounds the lament of old Atlas, in his solitude holding up the world:

> Ich unglückselger Atlas! eine Welt,
> Die ganze Welt der Schmerzen muss ich tragen. . . .[6]

We must help the old Titan. Loud-voiced Atlas, entwined by clouds at the horizon, where are you fleeing from us, together with the horizon, in order to lament again your solitude?

6. "I, unhappy Atlas! A world, the whole world of pain must I bear. . . ." (A Schubert song set to a poem by Heine).

The black profiles of the men in tails and their masks become as transparent as glass. Everything sinks into the ancient cosmic space. It is this space that eternally molds its dreams and makes suns spin.

Here world has fallen on world. And the cold planets have caught fire. Red tongues of fire erupt like red hair swirled by the wind.

And, over there, a solitary nebula is condensing, preparing at some point to give birth to suns, to eject a myriad of flaming jewels—red rubies and cosmic amethysts—onto the shore of time. Nations will war against nations amidst unchanging, unknown spaces. Then everything will settle down. The known will be overwhelmed by the unknown, and this city with houses, palaces, and temples will fly apart like an ancient phantom that has more than once troubled the quietude of Eternity.

What had seemed transparent and revealed the abyss of the world has faded again and reveals nothing. She stands there, an impulse grown mute. She is like a stately pine, crazy with grief and frozen in prayer.

But she leaves. A thunder of applause follows her. Aimless are the movements of a titan among dwarves. Great feelings and small deeds.

The masquerade starts again. Dresses rustle. Mask asks mask: "Well?" Mask answers mask: "Amazing."

Excited speeches and overly animated movements. A student has hurt his palms clapping too hard. The men in suits hop up, their tails streaming.

A *danse macabre* of the masks above the very same abyss.

When she sings, the depths of everything are revealed. But if you want to submerge yourself in those abysses, you still keep hitting a flat surface.

When will this end?

The Phoenix[1]

Egypt

The ancient face of the desert gazes out at you with a thought thousands of years old. The simoom whirls and swirls the curly locks of sand. The hundred-mouthed voices of the wind keep saying the same thing, the same thing. A smoky pillar of sand flies up, threatening with waterlessness and dryness this land of grace.

Egypt is a land of grace. Since time immemorial life has been waging a war with death here. And since time immemorial Typhon has been sailing in yellow clouds of sand and soaring and soaring and flying and flying in pillar after pillar like a stately palm: Brown palm forests surge unstoppably toward Egypt from the Sahara, inundating with sand the fertile fields. Thus, the desert beats the fertile body of Egypt. Egypt is the drum of the world, enormous, announcing the war of the sun against darkness.

Is it surprising that many of the religious mysteries contained in ancient Greek as well as Judaic culture have their roots in Egypt? From here the Phoenix of the religious fire has flown repeatedly, being reborn again and again from the ashes of history. The very doctrine of rebirth through resurrection has its deep foundation in Egypt.

How touching is the legend of that miraculous bird—the eagle-like Phoenix. Every 500 years the Phoenix flies from Arabia to Heliopolis to die. The Phoenix is a bird of the sun, consecrated to Osiris. The Phoenix is the very soul of the solar god.

Since time immemorial Egypt has stood at the boundary between life and death. Egypt created remarkable images signifying the triumph of death. At the edge of vast sands Egypt erected the stone body of the gigantic Sphinx. It is a symbol of the bestial past, a celebration of death.

But Egypt is also the cradle of lightning-like myths of the bright bird

1. First published in the magazine *Vesy*, 1906, no. 7. Some material in this essay has been omitted.

dying and rising from the dead on the third day, according to Scripture. This symbol already represents the religious tragedy of a suffering resurrection illuminating all cultures with a ray of the future. The Phoenix—eternal resurrection—melts the heavy past, burning everything with the fire of its luminous wings as with a radiant dawn. Dissipated are the sphinxes flying since time immemorial into the sacred land together with the yellow clouds of sand.

Since time immemorial the sphinxes have crisscrossed the azure of Egypt, like swallows squealing in the wind and cutting the air with their sharp purple screams. And perhaps more than once the Pharaoh directed his absent-minded gaze at them when he went out onto the palace steps to catch some fresh air, planning perhaps the execution of the Jewish children.

The Phoenix and the Sphinx

The Sphinx and the Phoenix are images of one battle. These images are characterized by an integral unity, represented either as the triumph of the past (the Sphinx) or as the triumph of the future (the Phoenix). The Sphinx and the Phoenix are opposed to one another. He who is able to transform the mystery of the Sphinx into nothing will understand that the Sphinx does not contain any mystery. He has at least once in his life seen the Phoenix's sparkling feather, flashing like bejeweled lightning on the horizon of our yearnings.

The Sphinx is, strictly speaking, a misunderstood Phoenix. She represents an aspiration to life without a valuable relation to life. The being of the true and valuable is replaced by being in general. Life becomes animal-like. The Sphinx and the Phoenix are, in essence, one symbol. But in the consciousness of one who contemplates them they are sundered into day and night, morning and evening, future and past, the feathery and winged and the immobile and stony. The Sphinx and the Phoenix are opposed to one another. They are antagonistic principles.

Revelation of the eagle word is opposed to revelation of the bestial word. But the Beast of the Apocalypse represents the final unriddling of the sphinxes. But the winged eagle of the Revelation of John clarifies the myth of the burning and resurrected Phoenix.

The eagle of the heights is a bird and every bird is a dragon. Magicians tell us that an eagle can be transformed into a dragon. But, conversely, in the dragon one can see certain traits of the bird.

This amounts to exorcising the demon from the bestial traits. The mystery of the Phoenix exorcises demons and teaches one to walk on water. He who believes in the mystery of the Phoenix "is not condemned: but he that believeth not is condemned already. . . . And this is the condemnation, that light is come into the world, and men loved darkness rather than light" (John 3:18–19). The Sphinx and the Phoenix battle against each other in our souls. And on all things produced by the human spirit lies the stamp of the Phoenix and the Sphinx. That is why in labors of thought, in works of art and science, and in social creativity the prophetic images of Egypt, the Phoenix and the Sphinx, are always resurrected.

In one direction they are opposed to one another. In another direction they are inseparable. The mystery consists in the fact that the Phoenix is not contained in the Sphinx. But, as for the Sphinx, she is half of the whole Phoenix. Consumed by fire, the Phoenix dies. The Phoenix becomes scattered ashes. The Phoenix dies. But the Sphinx is the triumph of the bestial past over the future. But the Sphinx is precisely death. And the Sphinx and the Phoenix both came for this. The Sphinx is the antagonist. Both battle against fate. One defeats fate by open antagonism, the other by love. And the Phoenix rises alive and whole. That is why the battle of the Sphinx with the Phoenix is not a battle of equal principles but a battle of parts with the whole.

It is a battle of life in general with creative life. But life in general flows from creativity. Life is part of creativity.

The Sphinx is half of the Phoenix. This halfness conditions the inevitable death of the Sphinx as a middle and separate principle.

Life and Creativity

Our contemporary theorists of knowledge separate norms of knowledge from forms of thought. They associate cognitive norms with the idea of the obligatory. Such a world-view establishes the practical character of cognition. But the idea of the obligatory grounds and predetermines being. This idea is not an existing or given category of thought. Being turns out to be subordinate to judgment. But judgment itself acquires a creative character.

"Let there be": this primordial act of creativity accompanies judgment. That is how it was on the first day of creation. That is how it is. That is how it will be. By this creating act the reasoning "I" is taken out of the domain of being. It is grounded outside of the images of life and death. The norm of the obligatory shapes creativity. The norm of the obligatory is the sole cognitive norm. Cognition turns out to be the eternal stellar fountain of created values. The shaped values reproduce before the creativity of the reasoning "I" a picture of the cosmic whole. Worlds and planetary systems arise. The history of nations arises. And out of the historical pictures of the past my personal "I" is born.

The personal "I" dissolves in valueless forms of animal life. It dies. But the subject of knowledge rises invariably in this unitary, impersonal, reasoning principle. This creative principle produces both the image of deity and the image of man.

The artist is the creator of the universe. The artistic form is the created world. Art begins new series of creations in the world of being. Because of this, art is separated from being. But in the artistic image the creative principle of being is blocked by the artist's personality. The artist is the god of his world. That is why the Divine spark that has fallen from the world of being into the artist's work imparts to the work of art a demonic gleam. The creative principle of being is opposed to the creative principle of art. The artist is opposed to God. He is eternally antagonistic to God.

The Sphinx of life is overcome, but it is overcome by another Sphinx, more terrible: by the Sphinx of the knowledge of good and evil. But one more step and the Sphinx of the knowledge of good and evil, who can turn into the devil and father of lies, is transformed into the Phoenix of life-giving creativity.

The norms of the obligatory are reducible to images of values. Only the experienced contents of consciousness can be valuable. But, previously, the content of consciousness was decomposed by science and psychology into mechanical components. These abstract components were united as a special kind of content of consciousness. The diverse grouping of contents of consciousness brings us to gnoseological concepts as the forms of these contents. The obligatory turned out to be a supraliminal norm linking liminal gnoseological forms.

But the obligatory must hang suspended in the void. The abstract thinking that predetermines being is then resolved, together with being, into nothingness. Or the obligatory is necessarily predetermined by the image of the experienced value. This final link (returning us from norm to being) of the progressing unity of forms of thought turns out to be, in essence, a unity of abstract and positive principles. It is a unity of word and flesh. It is resurrected value. It is union; it is symbol. We return to being. But being returns not in that narrow, limited sense in which it appeared to us before we sailed away into the land of thought. Being is henceforth taken not from the side of the past (the animal, fateful, physiological past) but from the side of the future (the integral, living, religious future). The Revelation of the Bestial Word is transformed into the Revelation of the Eagle Word. The eagle-like Phoenix rises before us from the scattered ashes of the Apocalyptic Dragon.

Our life becomes a value. We, as participants in a valuable life, dwell outside the limits of the old life and death. We can no longer die. Death and immortality are only ideas of our reason.

"And he led them out . . . and he lifted up his hands, and blessed them. And it came to pass, while he blessed them, he was parted from them, and carried up into heaven" (Luke 24:50–51).

The Mystery of the Phoenix

The Phoenix of resurrection and immortality has already burned our hearts with the fire above its grave, scattering the ashes of petrifaction and melting the sphinx countenance of our life. Now we—phoenixes—gently ascend from the earth. The growing capacity of our reason surrounds us like a blue celestial sea.

In the newly created world of being, the valuable world, we begin again and again the creative process. The created world of values is overcome again and again. Behind us it becomes petrified in forms of visible being with the history of states and nations. We perish again and again in this petrified world. That is why this world becomes for us nonexistent in the past. And we perish in it in order like phoenixes to rise on the third day in a new form.

If the Sphinx of the past describes before us an empty infinity, the Phoenix rises eternally above the infinity of worlds, never seeing the infinity of each of them.

If the Sphinx is the personification of the dark infinity of being and of chaos, the Phoenix is the personification of a different infinity, an eternally rising eagle infinity. The flight of creativity is uniquely directed by the mystery of the redemption of voluntary death in the created world for resurrection in the new world that is being created.

Fly, Phoenix, sun on resplendent wings! But do not dare grow weary! Do you wonder with horror, Phoenix, about what will happen to you when you realize that, no matter how many times you are resurrected, you will be scattered into ashes again and again? An infinite number of times you will fly to your bonfire and undergo the torments of burning.

But the Phoenix overcomes death by love. And as soon as the Phoenix says to death "Let there be," the eyeless companion of our days experiences horror and is scattered into nothingness like the Sphinx. And as soon as the Phoenix dons the red dawn of fire, the freshening wind whispers to him: "Returning, it's returning." And immortality on wings of peace will descend to the Phoenix, and he will rise on the third day, as Scripture says.

And the Phoenix will say: "My immortality has returned to me. It, it alone, gazes at me through life and death."

The Sage

You, sages who have become phoenixes. You walk along the Milky Way. The Milky Way is a handful of precious values scattered in the world. The Milky Way is a bridge cutting across the heavens. Beneath your feet is the precipice of horror. In order to step further, you create a new value. And by creating it, you overcome. And you create a new value. And by creating it, you overcome. Thus it continues without end, without end. Without end you create and you overcome.

You are comets, madly joyous, madly ripping apart from primordial times the fabric of the black darkness. Behind the shoulders of petrified history being itself is the feathery sparkling tail of a comet, the transparent robe of a flying sage. And from the infinite robe the darkness of the long night blooms infinitely.

The sage turns around to look at his robe, spread across the heavens like an airy winged sail. He recognizes the Milky Way. And the nebulae. And the planetary systems. Contemplating the folds of his robe, he recognizes everything. He recognizes the cosmic life of the planets. He recognizes the emergence of nations. He sees himself thrown into the whirl of being. He laughs to himself. He lovingly looks at himself. He calls: "Come unto me." And his distant call penetrates like a dawn into the dream where he dreams of himself. And this other he, trapped in the dream, dreams of the dawn and of someone's dear familiar voice, calling with restful tenderness: "Come unto me, all ye that labour and are heavy laden, and I will give you rest."[2]

Thus the sage contemplates the contours of his spreading robe. Thus the sage forgets himself, immersed in his dream. And he dreams of the infinity of being. But if he chances to turn his veiled countenance, there will unfurl before his gaze the picture of the constellations amidst which he is thrown in his jagged headlong flight.

The sage is a screaming red swallow, cutting across the void of night with its flight and its springtime song.

When the sage turns to look at his past, his feathery cloudlike robe is transformed for him into a petrified image of the Sphinx. The cloudlike contours, fluffed like feathers into the heavens, turn to stone.

2. Matthew 11:28.

But the Sphinx is only a contour on the Phoenix's blinding feathers. The Phoenix's dawn feathers are speckled like a peacock's feathers with the eyes of somber sphinxes. In the same way, the bright joyous dawn, speckled with dark little clouds, reminds us of a leopard's skin, stretched over the horizon.

The Leopard's Skin

The leopard's skin of the dawn wounds our heart with an unheard-of closeness. There—far away, far away—people hear from ancient times the final mystery, the mystery that unites life and death.

The leopard dawn rises both in the spirit's striving to attain eternal religious mysteries and in the passionate music of Gypsy romances. The ancient voice keeps singing to us about the same thing, the same thing. And if the fiery songs of the Gypsies have become banal, we love them not banally but with the dawn of resurrection and immortality. It is as if the ancient voice of Egyptian immortality, ripping apart the gray clouds of banality with a leopard dawn, is audible to us in the rips between the words. Here is your voice, O Egypt:

> In the ancient songs lives your young spirit
> As in a choir of youth. Ah, listen and understand:
> The old Gypsy woman still sings alone.[3]

And listening to the voice of Egypt transmitted to us over the centuries in the Gypsy songs, we say to ourselves: "Yes, yes. We listen and understand." All of us madly love Gypsy songs, in the same way that Pushkin, that seer of mysteries, loved them.

The dawn's velvet skin scatters a golden and crimson gleam over the heavens. The golden dawns of self-divinization and the red dawns of Golgotha are both contained in the dawn's leopard skin. And is it not the Phoenix of resurrection that flies through our soul when the leopard skin is stretched over the horizon? Was he not looking at this skin

3. From a poem by Afanasy Fet.

when the great musician overheard the leitmotif of *Parsifal*? And there is no doubt that Nietzsche was looking at it when he was sighing and yearning for a golden drop of the golden wine of happiness.

To overhear the same velvet voice that penetrates us together with the dawn, is this not to become a phoenix? At dawn all of us are phoenixes to small some extent. And if we become phoenixes just once in our lives, that means the mystery of the Phoenix is with us. The Phoenix loves us the way a bride loves her bridegroom. All velvet, she glides up to us stealthily and kisses us: the dawn is the dear, dear, dear mystery of the Phoenix.

And the trees rustle at dawn: "You are returning.... Announce yourself.... You are again the Phoenix.... You have risen from the ashes.... With flaming wing break the airy mirror of the heavens...."

"Who are you? Who?"

"It is I, I[4].... Be with me for a little time, be with me. Without me you dragged along in the desert. Above you soared Sphinxes like black swallows. Ah, in your heart you thought of executing yourself and your children. I summoned you, Phoenix. I summoned you. And you returned to your love.... Five-hundred years have passed.... I am with you again; I will clothe you in crimson fire. The fire will rip apart your body and I will scatter the ashes. But you will return to me on the third day."

That is what the trees whisper. Nobody around. The dawn fades and suddenly the past returns.

You remember, the distant summons penetrates you in your dream where you dream of yourself in infinite being, in the cloudlike robe blowing behind your shoulders. You turn your countenance away from your robe, and the maw of the world opens, this maw into which you are thrown in your jagged headlong flight.

And you fly like a screaming red swallow, cutting across the void of night with its flight and its springtime song.

4. The speaker is feminine.

The Phoenix Will Rise!

We awaited the Phoenix. From the sacrificial altar rose a tongue of flame. It waxed and waned, licking the clear air. Women wept, burying the one who was to be encircled with the flame. Women wept, holding in their arms the urns which were to receive his burnt ashes.

And the Phoenix came. And he climbed up on the bonfire, trampling with his bare feet the hot tongues of flame. His white robe fluttered apart in ashes and an iron hand gripped his heart. But his gray eyes saw the distances and he struggled manfully with his torment.

The white robe of the Phoenix Nietzsche fluttered apart but he received the crimson fire from the hands of eternity. This fire burned his body. And the women, like the spice bearers, gathered into the urn his scattered ashes.

The grave will open at the dawn of the third day. And he will emerge risen before us. He will see the weeping woman and he will say to her: "Why are you weeping, why are you weeping over me? Look: the grave is empty. I am with you now and forever, even though you are still in the world but I am no longer in the world. I have remained faithful to the earth. I have given my body to be burned. I have been scattered into ashes. But now I have risen, I have risen faithful to earth and to heaven."

Drunk with the wine of the dawn, he will lay upon us his most pure dawn-gilded morning hands. And we will disperse joyously, spreading the news that the yearned-for mystery has been revealed and that the Phoenix Nietzsche has risen from the dead.

The Mask[1]

Dedicated to Vyacheslav Ivanov

The Nocturnal Soul

It has been a long time since mankind has listened so attentively to the strings of the soul. Unexpected tendencies have been disclosed in our hidden thoughts. Strange labyrinths of experiences concealing the unknown have been revealed. Paths have been discovered where it had appeared there could be no paths. We have come to a fateful frontier beyond we will find either death or victory.

Those who have made their way into these labyrinths of experiences and are gifted with alertness are filled by the hidden fear that they might be attacked by a roaring frenzied minotaur, threatening to impale them, so imprudently courageous, with its sharp horns. And suddenly an extended moaning in the depths of the labyrinthine passages is heard, and the earth shakes from the trampling of the furious hooves. Another second and the bold hero will see ahead of him two bright lights, drilling the darkness.

Night, "somber as a hundred-eyed beast,"[2] has advanced upon us from mysterious depths. When a night storm rushes at us,

> Night thickens, like chaos over water.
> And forgetfulness, like Atlas, presses on the soul.[3]

Advancing upon us is "universal silence," about which the poet says:

> Who among us, in the universal silence,
> Has listened without anguish

1. First published in the magazine *Vesy*, 1904, no. 6. Some material in this essay has been omitted.

2. From Tyutchev's poem "Sand everywhere up to the knees..." (1830).

3. From Tyutchev's poem "A Vision" (1829). Tyutchev has "presses on the land" instead of "presses on the soul."

> To the hollow moans of the epoch,
> To the prophetic voice of farewell?
>
> It seems to us that the orphaned world
> Is besieged by inexorable Fate
> And that in our struggle with all nature
> We are left to ourselves...[4]

The most sensitive among us unconsciously plug up our ears to keep from hearing the night storms of the "moaning" epoch—the hollow roar of the silence, resembling the wails of the frenzied minotaur in the desolate darkness of the nocturnal labyrinths. We unconsciously avert our eyes from the depths and gaze instead at the surface of consciousness, though we know that we will inevitably reach those depths and that they are terrifying.

Smooth are the surfaces of consciousness but the horizon is agitated. A pillar of cloud has risen at the horizon with hollow thunder and a flash of lightning. Who will help? Who knows? But the sleepers are silent in their deep sleep. The decrepit elder, agitated by the violent rush of cold wind, turns over on his side and mutters in his sleep: "All is calm: go to sleep..." And he again falls silent into his blissful ignorance.

> The hour approaches when
> Somber night, like a hundred-eyed beast,
> Looks out from every bush[5]

and our frightened nocturnal souls are crazed in their anguish. The cold storm roars past in a furious charge, raising up the dust of the earth; and like a pillar at the horizon rises the deaf-mute blue Atlas, who has fallen on the land, covering it with forgetfulness.

4. From Tyutchev's poem "Insomnia" (1829).
5. See note 2 on p. 25.

Masks

There are beings who are strangely enigmatic. Sleepers do not suspect their existence, because for them these beings do not differ in any way from other people. But like bloodless phantoms, these masked changelings, gliding past, are visible to those of us who are awake. They know all things. They see all things. But they do not speak. Their eyes contain unending distances and their smiles are serpent-like. Their faces are wearing masks. Look: do you see how many masks have appeared among us? Forgotten terrors have returned to the surface of consciousness and the mask of ancient Greece has been resurrected.

Their eyes reflect only that at which they are directed. Where are they focusing their enigmatic eyes if these eyes are gashes against which abysses press? On their laughing lips, which are also full of terror, the midnight wind plays its solitary songs, their words thus causing a cold draft. There are those who have tasted the depths, but they have donned the mask of sleep and are silent about that which is deep, so that nobody will know what they hang suspended above.

Beneath the mask of the visible the invisible can be glimpsed. The mask fuses flatness with depth. That is why masks are marked by a symbol: someone deep has glanced into their thin countenance. We will never say who it is that is looking at us there, from beneath the mask, but we are frightened when we are observed by those who are masked.

It is said that the symbol is the kernel of the myth and that in creating a myth a genius will merge with the crowd.[6] The conspirators of the coming action are known by their masks.

The tragic mask, the symbol of the ripening action, is by its unspeakable appearance able to transform into a statue the one who looks at it, this mask with a halo of serpentine hair of the Gorgon who looks out at us from a horrible void.

That is why we begin to suspect that faces, however handsome they may be, are capable of infecting us with fear—that they are masks beneath which a Medusa horror is staring at us.

6. See Vyacheslav Ivanov's essay "The Poet and the Rabble." (Bely's note)

Action

The ineffable is silent. The need for communion with others does not vanish for those have come to know the depths of the ineffable. On the contrary, this need grows greater, because solitude is agonizing when we are observed from all directions by the watchful eyes of timelessness. The desire is to *see* together with others, to meet the depths together with others. Word does not have the power to express the ineffable, and so we turn to music. But music is a call to action. And to the extent that music expresses the unconditional foundation of being (will), it is an unconditional sign of action, an action which expresses being.

What is inexpressible by word can be expressed by action. The tragic mask that has appeared among us calls us, who have attained the knowledge, to a common action. A similarity of intoxications producing the whirl of psychic bursts—this similarity is the beginning of the action. The swirling whirl of separate experiences penetrating one another and fused by music into a purple Dionysian flame lifting the inflamed ones into the sapphire chalice of the heavens—is this whirl not capable of creating rituals of circular action, khorovods,[7] dances, songs?

There will again be days when on blossoming springtime meadows, amid violets and lilies of the valley, to the ecstatic howling of long pipes and the laughter of bells, youths clothed only in tiger skins and crowned with green leaves will whirl under the moon, sanctifying the great action with their chaste dance.

Friedrich Nietzsche

Words are shadows of experiences. By deepening an experience, we impede its transmission. In the soul there remains an excess of raptures and sufferings that cannot be transmitted to anyone:

7. Form of Slavic folk art combining circle dance with choral singing.

> How can the heart express itself?
> How can another understand you?
> Can he understand the things by which you live?
> A thought when uttered is a lie.
> Excavating them, you'll only muddy the sources.
> Drink from them and keep silent.[8]

Art no longer satisfies. Instead of bottomless images the soul demands bottomless life. Artists, poets, and musicians are those few who have access to the contemplation of the abysses. Meanwhile, when he represents the bottomless, an artist, instead of going into the abyss, goes away from it, contenting himself with the representation alone and liberating himself for new contemplations. Before him is a whirl of contemplations, not a whirl of actions. That is why the artist cannot be the leader of our life.

We seek a *different leader*, one who has passed silently over the abysses and concluded his path by finding repose on the other shore. From behind his tragic countenance, torn to shreds, emerges a new countenance, to be his forever—the countenance of a child who has found repose on the other shore, a countenance that gazes at us with a smile of gentle sorrow. The terrible and radiant countenance has been refined into transparence by joy, tenderness, and stillness.

In the last years of his life Nietzsche was quietly silent. Music would bring a smile to his tormented lips.

When we are beset by secret horrors and secret fears, none of those near us can bring us any consolation. The mad Nietzsche knew of course how to approach a person at times of secret peril and how to embolden him with a prolonged gaze without words.

Sometimes in a crowd on the street we catch a glimpse of transparently slender, immobile, pale-white features which glimmer before us like a hope or like a warning. You turn around to look and see only a back and a soft hat: the silhouette has vanished around the corner. And you don't know if you dreamt this vision or if it actually happened.

I imagine that somewhere on the street there is an elegant immobile silhouette, with pale face raised high and with soft blond whiskers,

8. From Tyutchev's famous poem "Silentium" (1830).

with a white top hat, and with a deep gaze, childlike and veiled with a kitten's softness as with a mist, but a mist in which the arrows of a tiger's wrath could flash. I imagine a hand wearing a tight-fitting glove and holding a red Morocco leather briefcase—the vision of a silhouette gliding amid the streets.

On the other side of the street two students are running along. They lift their hats respectfully and he, taken by surprise as if awakened from a deep sleep, lifts his white top hat with an ingratiating courtesy. One passerby says to another: "It's Herr Professor Nietzsche..."

Arthur Nikisch[9]

Arthur Nikisch has a strange face. He rises quietly to the podium, slowly surveys the musicians with a pensive gaze, carefully raises his hand (as if quieting the roar of storms that have not yet arrived), and draws himself erect like a string. Suddenly he is transformed and elicits thunderous sounds in which we hear

> ...the hollow moans of the epoch,
> ...the prophetic voice of farewell.

His elegant white hand seems to swim and melt in the air, and how significant then is the look of this face with its squinting eyes! Pale, pale, with tousled hair falling over his brow and with a graying goatee: it's as if you've somehow already seen this age-old face when he was pulling himself out of the somber waves of chaos with a sad little smile, warning us of labyrinths of horror. And here once again the old face of our childhood dreams has appeared, signifying the return of forgotten delirium...

And now, growing completely still, he stretches out his hands and then quickly lowers them, becoming still again, as if he had broken off a drunken hysteria of sounds. And then rises the symphony's fateful leitmotif from out of the ancient labyrinths.

9. See note 5 on p. 10.

Here, as before, with frenzied roar rushes the minotaur, breaking all the heart's hopes.

Night thickens, like chaos over water.
And forgetfulness, like Atlas, presses on the soul.

The Man Possessed by Frenzy

Visions stretch above the abysses of the spirit.

It is as if we hear the screams of a man possessed by frenzy who has smashed his reed-pipe against a cliff: "I am now alone! Why do you make me drunk, O sun, maker of wine? I have forgotten everything! The abyss has opened its silent maw! I feel strange! Where am I? There is no one here! Everything is gone—vanished!"

Birds, those screaming trumpets of rapture, whirl white-breasted above him and cry out their notes. Cosmic atoms emit their light. The light has inundated everything! Steams of light have pierced his greedily breathing breast. Streams of light have entered his heart—golden arrows, golden!

A leopard's skin sways behind the shoulders of the man possessed by frenzy. In his dance he has pressed thorns to his pale white brow. His pale white brow is torn by thorns. He is bleeding. And he screams, rejoicing: "I do not exist! I do not exist! My blood has turned to wine! Come to me and drink; come to me and torture me

you who are illuminated

with the evening light; transmute the blood's purple into wine, into golden sunset drunkenness—

transmute it, O you who are wine-purple!"

He was drunk with happiness. But he opened his soul to the sunset and a brightly purple flame descended on him. This was the burning wick of sweet-smelling springtime ethers.

The Clearing

When the sinister birds, keening, rush at you and the blue crowds of Atlases slouch toward you like mountains—know, then, you nocturnal souls who conceal storms within you, know that you shall taste the sweetness of immeasurable bliss. No one who is afraid of storms and death will know that bliss. Give yourself to all winds, to all storms—O nocturnal souls!

A violent blue giant descends upon you from the wine-golden sky. He swings a thundering cliff at you. His smoky arms are raised to the evening heavens.

Nocturnal souls who conceal storms within you—do not be afraid!

Woven of the silky tenderness of clouds, the thundering giant will pour out in golden rain. Sparkling with streams of dawn gold, he will return to the sea that gave him birth—

to the great sea

whose turquoise sigh tore him away from the waters and carried him into the heavens as a ball of pale-blue thunder.

The Song of Life[1]

Art (*Kunst*) is the art of living. To live is to know how, to know, to be able to (*können*). Knowledge of life is the ability to preserve all life (my own, that of others, that of the clan or community). But the preservation of life consists in its continuation; the continuation of anything at all consists in acts of creation; art is the creation of life. The instrument of creative activity is knowledge; knowledge separated from creative activity is an instrument without the one who wields it; such an instrument is a purposeless instrument; such knowledge is dead knowledge.

Nevertheless, this form of uncreative knowledge is dominant in our culture.

Therefore, it faces the threat of death.

Our culture dues not know life; it does not want life; it cannot live. But our culture is the crown of the various kinds of human knowledge. This crown is a crown of death. Humankind faces the threat of death.

This is not a fantasy: Humankind is in fact degenerating. Bad heredity reigns everywhere; the very condition of egoistic regeneration, i.e., the normality of sex, is collapsing.

Finally, there are certain facts that compel us to see degeneration in changes of the human skeleton (e.g., the reduction of the number of chest vertebrae). All these external symptoms are signs of the degeneration of the human soul and of its life-rhythm.

Originally, art as the creation of life-values is the production of healthy offspring outside oneself or the accumulation of life force within oneself. The first pathway of art is the transformation of the species. The second pathway is the transformation of the person; on this pathway, art and religion are one.

The first pathway (the transformation of life outside oneself) is the pathway that humankind has followed, and it has led humankind to self-negation. How did this happen?

The root of art lies in the person's creative power which grows in

1. First presented as a lecture at the House of Song on 6 November 1908.—Trans.

the battle against the surrounding darkness. Darkness is fate, and the person's task is to overcome fate whatever form it may take: e.g., the form of bears attacking people (which was common in the cave period) or the form of an evil spirit threatening people. Here, in this dark prehistoric period, the creation of a harmonious person (a hero) is a necessary condition of life; here, life is a drama and the person is its hero; here, life is creative activity and art is life. And artistic form is the person hewing ladders out of life where the steps are moments; subordinating the moment to himself, the person passes his self-consciousness through a series of moments. The form of the manifestation of the person is then separated from the person; the sum of the moments is the sum of artistic forms: the person is one. Thus, the forms of life (i.e., the artistic forms) are separated from the person; man is an artist of many forms. The notion of form becomes more complex: form in the strict sense ("I" expressed in the body) becomes the creative principle of forms in the figurative sense (instrument, clothing, habitation, thought). Here, art in our sense is united with the applied character of instruments of production: the spear is decorated, clothing is arrayed with feathers, pictures are painted in the habitation, thought is embodied in the form of song, myth, and image. The process of creative activity (i.e., life) which had been experienced as the hero's creative song becomes now an artifact of creative activity.

Kunst becomes *techne*.

Artifacts change into products. The transformation of creative forms establishes a system of mutual aid of creative activity: the hero who had overcome fate by the creation of life becomes now a soldier-warrior protected by creative artifacts; the form of life, like armor, encircles the person's rhythm: fate, chaos, the bear, or the evil spirit no longer penetrate the defense that encircles the community: creative activity becomes the creation of idols, and the idol protects the community from the darkness of night. The idol now demands the sacrifice of the person and of the person's rhythm; the slaughter of the sacrifice is grounded in the fear that if the hero (now the soldier) wishes to return to his heroic past, this past, having been transformed into the hero, threatens to destroy the encircling defense made of images and lets darkness (the bear or the evil spirit) into the previously invulnerable habitation: courage dries up and life-rhythm becomes attenuated.

And since the hero resides in everyone, everyone experiences an unfamiliar coercion: the coercion not of the demon but of the fetish or idol; this idol's name is the security of the clan or community. The images here are products which replace creative value. The fetishism of product-creation, the creation of idols and forms of art, the coercion of the hero—all these things are personifications of the same attenuation of the rhythm of life.

The replacement of creativity by comfort liberates the instruments of production (thoughts, the objects of consumption, etc.): everything is adapted to general use. The source of creativity (the person), expressed in motion, is replaced by products of the person, by dead copies; and imperceptibly a corpse (the fetish) is enthroned over life. That is the origin of the state with its law and morality; it is also the death of the nature of religion and creativity: in man the living "I" becomes a fruitless contemplation of the surrounding nature and even of one's own nature; this second step of the participation of life consists in the rich development of philosophy and science.

In the past, the creativity of life, governed by rhythm, not only healed the artist's nature but also established in him the ladder of transformations; the allegorical picture of these transformations was reflected in biology as the origin of animal species, while religious images, songs, dances, and prayers were means for hewing new steps in the ladder of the universe: Man was ascending from earth to heaven, and he would already be in heaven if thought had not transformed the song of earth and heaven into unnatural abstractions, if it had not transformed earth into the concept of the law of nature and heaven into the norm of the reasoning consciousness.

This two-fold deadening of rhythm (first in law and morality and then in science and philosophy) enchained life in a heavy armor. The creativity of life ceased to exist, though it is true that history witnessed the rise of titans who shook the world to its foundations, as if they were throwing weights around, but soon those titans too ceased to exist, for the weights became too heavy for these heroes. Humankind stopped being agitated by the volcano of personal creativity, and the species, as the sum of enslaved persons, withered without the necessary creative exercise and the mechanism governing the world—the invisible corpse—instead of human beings spewed out millions of marionettes:

the person, fallen into deep sleep, became a marionette and the person's life became a movie. Every personification of the hero's image and likeness disappeared from culture. The fetish itself disappeared, having disintegrated into a series of logical judgments—of norms suspended in the void. Science fragmented the fetish into atoms and lines of force; philosophy derived the laws of force-generation from the laws of word-generation: Humankind now is only a letter; the hero is a letter ("X," "Y"); society consists of words composing logical conclusions, but the conclusions lack a person who concludes: Something is thought and something is created—that is the result of contemporary philosophy, the completion of the degeneration. We are even forbidden to be curious about the identity of that invisible one who thinks us, making us what we are.

This enormous and extreme degeneration of the world is not an imagining but a brief summary of the world-views of the pillars of the two most consistent theories of knowledge: Cohen and Husserl.

There's nothing left but to sit down comfortably with hands folded in one's cabinet, to fall asleep and then die.

That is what we have made out of the creativity of life. As long as we thought that the struggle with fate was our task, tragic forces ejected onto the surface of life the fiery lava of religion and of the forms of art. So, we have now obediently folded our hands: If the supra-individual norm of knowledge draws for us a picture of time and space and of us passing through time, all this according to the laws of the reasoning consciousness which thus in general is thought in itself—then even the struggle with fate is predetermined by fate.

Thus, fate devoured us even before the creation of the world.

The history of culture is the history of the development of forms of production—of thoughts, objects of consumption, social relations, etc., i.e., of artifacts of creativity where the creator is equated to zero, so that "the development of society is goal-oriented" (that is what we are taught) but the goal of the development is a naked thought, a fiction: "progress," "the state," and so on. The means, however, are living flesh and blood: the fiction devours hecatombs of human sacrifices, as if power is sacrificed to what does not exist. The artifact devours the artificer, and the rhythm of life no longer has a point of application in life, so that the essence of life becomes an essence outside of life, and doctrines of eternal life outside of life, somewhere in the clouds, are developed: the tricky Jesuits of thought put God in heaven and leave earth to Moloch. Whatever names these Jesuits of culture might give themselves (mystics, theologians, or atheists), their role is always the same: they are executioners of life.

When participating in the lawgiving of life, the goal-orientedness of personal development is a goal-orientedness without any goal. Such was the Jesuitical definition of art offered by that corpse of genius, Kant, who affirmed in the forms of art the unnatural manifestation of the rhythm of life when there remained no place for rhythm in life; rhythm created for itself forms outside of life; those forms were the forms of the arts; and the fable of the celestial heights of art got started, but those celestial heights are the pulsing of the blood and the beating of the heart. The goal of art is to blow up the sleep of life. The statesmen of philosophy prevent art from doing this; they prevent it by formulating the theory of goalless goal-orientedness.

If our life is cultural death, then somewhere at a distance from life we find the life of creativity. Humankind begets a form of art in which the world is melted in rhythm so that earth and heaven cease to exist and there is nothing but the melody of the universe. This form is the musical symphony. Outwardly, this form is the maximally perfect form of distancing from life; inwardly, it touches the essence of life—rhythm. Therefore, we call the rhythm of life the spirit of music: here we find the prototypes of ideas, of worlds, of beings. Here the artist is a spirit soaring above the chaos of sounds in order to form a new world of creativity and with this world to crush the creative fragments called being: the task of rhythm is rip apart heaven and to crush the earth; it is to throw heaven and earth into the abyss of non-being, because the artist's soul contains a new heaven and a new earth: "Death . . . [is] cast into the lake of fire,"[2] as the voice of Revelation tells the Apostle. "It is already cast"—somewhere in the depths of the soul, and therefore in the depths of the soul the song of triumphant life already resounds; but we pollute the soul with creative refuse; we do not understand the

2. Rev. 20:14.

voice; we do not know that "death is cast into the lake of fire." The music must pour into our blood so that our blood becomes music; and we will then understand that transfiguration is within us and immortality is with us.

But deep is the sleep: We are even incapable of thinking rhythmically; we only have dreams of imaginary flying shells: we forget that there is nowhere for us to fly away from ourselves. Let us fly away; let us all become zeppelins: a flying zeppelin is a dream of flight, and flight on an airplane is a hyperbolic flight. Flight is not a comfortable displacement from one point of space to another. Flight is ecstasy, enthusiasm, the being consumed by fire; if ecstasy raptures our body too, we agree to be "birds in the air";[3] but as long as we play with airplanes, the birds have every right to laugh at us.

The separating out of forms from the musical (nocturnal) element of the soul—that is the cosmogony of art. First, there was the advancing period of art; this was a prehistoric period; the musical element of night sang out nameless cries in the savage, and the symbol of this nocturnal song was the night surrounding primitive man: "an incorporeal and invisible world seethed in the nocturnal chaos."[4] For the savage the sky of the soul and the celestial dome were one and the same. The hero fought against incorporeal spirits as well as against bears; he advanced and triumphed, and the line of his nocturnal path was illumined by the light of the emerging images. Images, life-routines, and idols of thought were the trophies ripped out of the hands of night; at the moment when the hero reposed upon the trophies, surrounding himself with images, it was then that history, i.e., the hero's dream, arose: the ocean of night penetrated into the continent of images and the hero built from the images a citadel (laws, right, the state), thus making a fetish responsible for the defense of his life instead of understanding that the battle against fate is the battle against one's own inertia, for only that kind of battle carves new steps in the ladder of the universe.

3. *Birds in the Air* (1908) is a book of poems by Konstantin Balmont.

4. From a poem by Tyutchev.

In that period, when man transformed the creative step into the plane of being, that plane became the infinity of this life and the hero became a wanderer over the plane of infinity. Thus, humankind changed the line of its path; the line of the previous path continued into heaven; it became the heaven suspended above man. And earth became the new path.

That was the beginning of the period of defensive art: it was necessary to veil the celestial abyss with images and that's where mythology came in: a carpet of images was stretched over the abyss; the Olympian day appeared; the continent of earth, protected by gods, grew stronger, and historical culture developed.

Here the person split apart into spirit (or rhythm), soul (or light fragmented into colors, i.e., paints where the sky is the palette), and body. Out of the body separated the inertia of the earth, represented in art as architecture and sculpture. Out of the soul separated the sky, light, and paints, i.e., the art of painting. Out of the spirit separated song, splitting apart into poetry and music. Thus grew the world of the arts—Apollo's golden carpet stretched over the musical abyss.

Song begets poetry; rhythm forms poetic meter; the complexity of meter engenders poetic prose, i.e., style. Style transfigures word; the forms of the transfiguration of the word are the means of representation. Such is poetry from the side of the word; from the side of content, it is the vision of a god; primordially, the poetic myth is based on the appearance of a god to a bacchante, a priest, or a sorcerer; and the continuation of the image in imagination, i.e., in rhythm, changes the hallucination. The vision takes different forms: rhythm multiplies the images; the relation of the parts of the sundered image to the image is a relation of thesis and antithesis to synthesis; the thesis is again fragmented into thesis and antithesis and so on and so forth. And the result is a system of images, or a myth; that is the origin of religion. The laws of the fragmentation of images are laws of numbers: out of myth originate kabbalistics, mathematics, and celestial mechanics. Here we find the roots of Pythagoreanism. The content of song splits apart, on the one hand, into logic, metaphysics, and science; and into morality on the other hand. Religion becomes dogmatics; religious renewal comes only through mysticism when the latter attempts to re-transform dogma into symbol. Religious gnosticism, theosophy, and metaphysics emerge; the whole diversity of rhythmic modulations of song is formed; the musical pathos of the soul becomes the content of religion, poetry, and metaphysics.

The expulsion of content from religion leads to symbolic absurdity, i.e., to scholasticism.

The expulsion of content from poetry leads to rhetoric. Its expulsion from metaphysics leads to the theory of knowledge; here the word is free of all psychism. But the word is always a symbol; when the word is affirmed in the metaphorical (not figurative but formal) sense, we demand to know to what the word has been transferred; but the object of the word is absent. Such is the fate of terms; a term is a word bereft of content; the theory of knowledge is the death of the living word. Life hides in the wordless; the transformation of words into terms is a special form of muteness as well as the beginning of the revolt of chaos in our soul, the approach of a new deluge. In emptying the word, science and philosophy kill the half-alive, decaying words of numerous scholastics and metaphysicians; bad words die: we are liberated from all illusory life (and in our culture this life consists in the life of words).

We listen to the song without words.

Now we begin to understand that all of these norms of knowledge by means of which the nonexistent thinks its complement (which turns out to be us ourselves) are just collections of words. We rapturously adorn the theory of knowledge with wreaths of our reverence, for our gnoseological tendency is our final tribute to a corpse; when we are metaphysicians, we dig corpses (philosophical systems) out of their graves; when we call ourselves gnoseologists, we bury the corpse (the philosophical system), thus opening a path to future creativity.

We have even invented a special logical form in which we bury every logic; on the basis of logic we affirm logic as a form of creativity; through this affirmation Kant's universally obligatory judgments are thrown back into the past. Our path is music as a norm; our future is music as a value.

The highest value of the theory of knowledge is that it teaches us to perform mental *saltos mortales*: a bad word, having completed its circle of development, will without delay bite its own tail like a snake.

Philosophy predetermined knowledge by creativity; people listened to the voice of creativity, but no words were found; music sang out and mixed everything up. The connection joining words, names, and images to one content or another fell apart; instead of life, we had movies; instead of feelings, we had chaos; instead of ideas, we had melody; instead of history, we had style. All was only music; to hear it was to understand all, but to understand was to create; investigation of the epoch became a form of creative improvisation; history ceased to exist. The one, resounding as rhythm in time, as tonality in space, as melody in causality—that was the mood of the first symbolists at the end of the 19th century: Colors sang out, the line flew, thoughts were scattered; people began to think in vitrages of the 18th century and in ornament; scientific methodology became symbolic (this was not a loss but a gain for science); religious dogmas were transformed into creative leitmotifs; the history of culture and the history of art were enriched by valuable works, but interest in the historical works increased in proportion to the loss of the sense of historical distance: Goncourt had just started listening to the song of Japanese painting when Manet resurrected it in his art; this was followed by works of Gonze, Revon, Tomkinson, and others devoted to the Japanese, and Aubrey Beardsley recreated our epoch à la japonaise in order to bring it close to Watteau. Beardsley and especially Redon became true visionaries.

Colors sang out: in Rimbaud sounds became colors; in Verlaine words became sounds. Deussen infinitely enriched German orientology, and Nietzsche resurrected Greece; all times and all spaces became notes of a single scale, but the tonality of the scale was a blessed land dissolved in azure: the land where heaven and earth are one; and as long as this land was understood as a dream where the past will be resurrected in the future and the future lives in the past but where the present does not exist, Watteau's symbolic painting *L'Embarquement pour Cythère* became the slogan of creativity and the 18th century came back to life in utopias. This unconscious trembling means we are conscious of the indisputable reality of our forefathers' utopias in the land of dream. The needle of Nietzsche's compass points toward Dream which turns out to be Eternity.

Watteau comes to life before us in a new way. Like the fantasist Beardsley, he frightens us with a harlequinade of masks, as for example in *Harlequin jaloux*. But when in *L'Embarquement pour Cythère* the song of the ship flies to the blessed isle, where a goddess rises out of the sacrificial smoke, we begin to see reality in Dream and nothing but dream in reality, as for example in *Les Plaisirs du Bal*. And life here is a song without words, like Verlaine's *Romances sans paroles*. Here, Verlaine, set to the music of Fauré, reminds us of the pale-blue Watteau.

Here, the heavens are transparent and the earth is not earth in the lunar azure: the fountains sing, gurgle, sob, and laugh; and rainbows too laugh in them. A boy embraces his girl; masks have come from somewhere, but one should not be frightened. Heaven and earth are not heaven and earth here in the lunar azure where tears sing, gurgle, sob, and laugh.

Masks have come from somewhere...

Our everyday life surrounds us with thousands of objects of luxury; with its bridges, towers, and railroads it protects us from the invasion of the unknown. It is the final manifestation of song, the final degeneration of rhythm on the path of song's evolution. Now song is changing the course of its flow. And everyday life is collapsing.

All of culture has grown out of songs and dances.

But as song degenerated, artful poetry blossomed in fabulous flower, philosophy wove its fine lace of thought from Medieval scholasticism to our own time, science gifted us with subtle instruments, and social relations manifested an intricate complexity. All this was a blossoming from the dying popular song.

Music separated itself from song and plunged into the depths of the soul; and from somewhere the symphony grew, but its place is in the concert hall, i.e., between four walls, and its symbols are the ball gown and the electric lamp.

Word separated itself from song, evolving in all directions and forming a garden of poetic forms with its finest flower being drama; but the theater fell with its stone vaults on drama and crushed it.

The word lit up with a thousand colors. History glistened with paradisal songs of colors from Beato's frescos to—placards: soon the artist will become a painter of posters.

Architecture became an engineering art: the building of bridges, American wheels, and towers became the artist's task.

In short: the market caused the degeneration of the matter of art; the spirit of art degenerated into theories of knowledge and science. Where green meadows once grew, we now find wastelands of sand.

Everyday life is given over to the movies and café-bars. History is a museum-panopticum.

Beneath the ugly scab of life Nietzsche heard the rhythm of life. The spirit of Dionysus was the name he gave to the beating of life and the spirit of Apollo was the name he gave to the life of the creative image. Both principles turned out to be outside of life, because life had ceased to be life; that is why we can define music only as the heaven of the soul and poetry as the clouds in this heaven. Out of heaven falls the cloud and out of rhythm falls the body—the union of rhythm with image. The symbol of the fusion of body with soul: the path indicated here returns to heroism, i.e., to the salvation of humankind: removed is the defense against chaos, a defense made up of dead images, thoughts, and knowledge. Culture collapses; the bear or the evil spirit again attacks us; but image and grotesque imagelessness, light and darkness—symbols of the soul's splitting apart—are the two branches of the tree of the knowledge of good and evil. The battle of man against fate is the battle of the hero against his own sleep; the tree of the knowledge of good and evil has a single trunk of life. The return to this single trunk is the motto of the future; the flow channel of life is deepened; the previous channel turns out to be imaginary, and culture with its towers of iron, with its knowledge and philosophy, turns out to be an illusion: its towers are cloud towers—they melt and collapse into the darkness. We have already received a whiff of the primordial crudeness and beauty of heroism from *Der Ring des Nibelungen*; we find there a song of our future, where Siegfried again battles Wotan (the bear[5]) and Wotan roams the earth in the form of a wanderer. Heaven will again be united with earth, and gods and men will roam freely—the men in heaven and the gods on earth.

History has transformed the tree of life into the tree of the knowledge of good and evil, and the hero has split apart into contemplator and doer. The doer produces goods; the contemplator glides above him in a cloud of thoughts. The doer is a slave and the contemplator is a god

5. The identification of the bear with Wotan appears to be an invention of Bely's.

and king; to be a slave in the image of divinity—that is our vocation in historical culture. The god in us has turned out to be a slave of his own sleep.

The cloud of thoughts is good; the products of life are evil. Morality has proclaimed detachment from the world, thereby offering man as a sacrifice to things. "Both your evil and your good are dead," proclaims Nietzsche and summons us to Dionysus, i.e., to the tree of life.[6] Others too saw in Dionysus an image of the tree soul, a dendritic soul. The Dionysian symbol is resurrected in the Jewish symbol of the tree of life; this means that the source of this tree is music. It is clear that music is the chaos out which (according to Boehme) God is born. The union of the god Dionysus with the symbolic tree of life deepens our understanding of the essence of religious symbolics. Vyacheslav Ivanov finds the same thing in Creuzer's theosophical symbolics and in the fantastic tales of Gottfried Keller. A Spencerian view of religion as the worship of ancestors encounters a Dionysian interpretation of religion in Rohde's *Psyche*.[7] Dionysus was originally a god of tree vegetation—*uleesis*, *phleon*; a "bacchus" is a young spruce sprout used as a decoration at Dionysian feasts. The tree is the original fetish, for it is the habitation of the soul (i.e., of music). And that is why the Biblical tree of life is a symbolic image of music. All this becomes clear after Nietzsche's *Geburt der Tragödie*. In this work Nietzsche relies on philology, on Burckhardt's investigations, and on Wagner and Schopenhauer, as well as on the voice of his own soul.

And the romantics come back to life before us in a new way: Joel[8] correctly points out that Nietzsche was born in the homeland of romanticism; he steeped himself in Novalis, saw Hölderlin's *Hyperion* as the prototype of the superman, and enjoyed the friendship of his teacher Koberstein, a historian of romanticism. Rohde detects traces of romanticism in ancient Greece. After Nietzsche we have a better

6. I have taken the following ideas in this paragraph from Vyacheslav Ivanov's remarkable study, *The Religion of the Suffering God*. (Bely's note)

7. See Erwin Rohde's *Psyche: Seelencult und Unsterblichkeitsglaube der Griechen* (1894).

8. See Karl Joel's *Nietzsche und die Romantik* (1905).

understanding of Tieck when the latter says: "all is a game." And going further, back into the depths of history, we encounter the philosopher of music Heraclitus, the Orphics, and the Pythagoreans. "I venerate fire," Schlegel echoes Heraclitus. "Let us write like the troubadours," exclaims Nietzsche. "Let us be bacchantes," proclaims Novalis.

And out of the musical pathos of the soul is born the dawn of a new wisdom, entirely bypassing the theory of knowledge: thought begins to play and sing; aphorism explodes into being.

All his life Nietzsche wrote about Dionysus, but he calls us to music in different ways: first he calls us to Wagner. Wagner derives from art the life of the future; the separate forms of art are for him an Egypt out of which he—a Moses—leads the chosen. But Wagner does not lead us to the promised land; instead, he abandons us in a desert of esthetic eclecticism.

So, Nietzsche abandons Wagner. He calls us to music, bypassing art: he invites us to sing our lives. He is a Noah building an ark-song at the moment when our ancient consciousness is threatened by a deluge of music: One cannot flee with impunity the living water; Nietzsche himself perished in the deluge; music flooded his consciousness. But we already know what Ark was built by Nietzsche: Song as an exercise in the rhythm of life—that is the path of the future. We must learn how to sing our lives.

Song is a symbol: image comes out of rhythm; a symbol is always real because it is always musical; and music is the living element of creativity. Out of song evolved poetry too, as well as music as a form of art; song is therefore the origin of all later complexification of images and rhythms. Its history is the history of the evolution of images: song is the musical connection of images. At the basis of religion, song is like prayer; at the basis of poetry, it is like lyricism; at the basis of music, it is like the point of origin of pure rhythm. Word here evokes image; word becomes image; word seeks flesh in order to become flesh; word creates the flesh of the life of harmony; word is rhythm, making image come out of the eternal element of the soul.

Rhythm is like the wind cutting through the heavens of the soul, like the wind born in the heavens, for the soul is the eternal proto-mother of the body and heaven is the eternal proto-mother of earth; out of the celestial abyss were born nebulae with their suns and their earths. The spirit of music reposed above the chaos; and there was light—the first day of creation; and earth was born out of heaven.

This first day of creation is approaching now, when we speak of new life-creativity. The deluge of music which is now ripping apart all the forms of life will be the first day: it will wash away the old world, and song will be the ark taking us on waves of chaos to the new creative life; word in song has the character of an invocation. We've forgotten that song is magic, and we'll soon learn that if we don't draw around ourselves a magic circle of songs, we'll perish in the deluge of music, in the musical deluge about to engulf all of culture. The horizon of our future is already covered with clouds; at this horizon the old chaos looks threatening and is flashing its lightning. The old chaos is slouching toward us: the deluge is coming.

Song is the first day of creation, the first day of the world of the arts. The musical element of the soul, in which everything is full (as in Thales) of "gods, demons, and souls," is illumined in song. And out of song come the forms of the arts; the earth of art comes out of the heaven of the arts; flesh comes out of soul.

Rhythm is the first manifestation of music; it is a wind agitating the blue ocean with ripples of cloud; clouds are born of collisions of winds. The cloudy haze of poetry is produced by the complexity of the soul's musical rhythms.

Just as in the shape of a cloud we detect the shapes of familiar images, so, in the same way, creative images are born out of the musical mist, where colors are tonalities and matter is the power and pitch of sound.

When we say, this is not a cloud, it is a giant, or a mountain ridge, or the unknown palace of an unknown city, we pull images of creativity down to the earth: the images, distancing themselves from music, become more ideal; but as they approach the earth they are perceptually—visibly—more real: in their nearness they are remote; in their remoteness (in music) they are near. Here, like Adam, we name images *with the names of things*. Images of fantasy also populate our world; this is the beginning of mythic creativity in art, the revelation of eternal reality in art.

But neither visibility nor fantasy is the life-element in song. Its life-element is music, whose ethereal heaven creates both our old earth and the new earth of our yearning.

Song unites rhythm (time) and image (space) in word (causality).

In a series of causes and effects creativity begins a new series of causes and effects: in a world of being it creates a world of values.

Song was the beginning of creativity in art. But now that creativity in art is more and more becoming the creation of dead forms, song is the first call to create living forms: it is a call to man, summoning him to become an artist of life.

Song calls. Song lives: Let historians study the laws of the multiplication and migration of songs. Let them teach us how French song migrated to Italy and Spain, how the sonnet and ballad crystallized out of song, how the poet Dante came out of the troubadours, and how in Greece Terpander's seven-stringed lyre begot melody, melody begot the strophe, and the strophe begot the great lyric poets of antiquity. We do not seek a systematic theory; we compose our living life in song. We, precursors of the future, may be insignificant, but we do know one thing:

Song lives and people live by song. They experience song; this experience is Orpheus and the image evoked by song is the shade of Eurydice—no, not the shade, but resurrected Eurydice herself.

In the image of Orpheus mythology imparted power to music, setting in motion the inertia of matter. Song is the actual world, transfigured by music, as well as the imagined world, transformed in music into Eve.

Song is the earthly isle, washed by waves of music; song is the habitation of children, washed by the ether of the sea—it is the isle to which Zarathustra called us. He called us to remain faithful to the earth.

Song is the one that is revealed in multiplicity. It is the *hen kai pan*, the one that forms out of all songs one song, the song of songs. It is love, for in love is contained creativity and in creativity is contained life. It is not by accident that the "Song of Songs" opens with the One Countenance of the beloved—of beloved Eternity, the sole beloved of Nietzsche, the prophet of earth. Revelation shows us the same countenance in heaven as well: we call this countenance the bride. Songs of earth and songs of heaven form the bridal veil of the Bride of eternity:

Nietzsche's eternal return and the return of Eternity—are they not the same thing? "The ring of rings, the ring of the return"[9]—is this not a wedding ring?

We know that when we sing we remain faithful to the earth in heaven as well; and remaining faithful to the earth, we love heaven: Where, if not in heaven, is our old earth?

We know now that soul and body are one, just as we know that earth and heaven are one; but we also know now that the earth of our soul and the heaven of our body are only creativity, and that the domain of creativity is not the distant isle Cythera, but life itself. We also know that not everything in life is life and that not all art is creativity.

Contemporaneity has made wise with the experience of audacity the innovators of art who attempted from the union of the forms of artistic creation to find a form illuminating the depths of life-strivings. The union of these arts lies not in the union of poetry with music; we have understood that sufficiently.

The highest point of music, its most complex form, is the symphony. The highest point of poetry, its most complex form, is the tragedy. It is impossible to unite livingly the symphony and the tragedy, just as theater united with the concert hall cannot be regarded as life. What does the mystery revealed to us in life have in common with Wagner's mystery with its ring and bells?

Poetry and music need to be united within us, not outside of us. We want to live by an actual, not reflected, unity of word and music. We want the temple of the arts to be crowned not by a dome, a dead form, but by man, a living form. Song is news of human transfiguration, and in our experiences this transfiguration unfolds a unitary and integral path. On this path, through the transfiguration of visible things we attain our own transfiguration. Our flesh is being melted as if in a crucible, though it appears to us that it is the world that is being melted. Here, in deeds, words, and feelings, man is the Minnesinger of his own life; and life is song.

But in the Minnesinger we recognize man transfiguring his own life. And his song is news of transfiguration. And if humanity is approaching a boundary of culture beyond which it will encounter either death

9. From *Thus Spoke Zarathustra*.

or new forms of life, it can hear its own fate in song and only in song. And we begin the song of our life.

We have forgotten how to fly. We think heavily and walk heavily; the heroic is lost to us and our life-rhythm is attenuated. Only when we regain lightness, divine simplicity, and health, will we be able to sing boldly our life, for if living life is not song, then life is not life.

We need a musical program of life separated into songs (heroic deeds), but we do not have a single song of our own. This means that we do not have our own order of soul and that we are not we at all but someone's shadows. It means that our souls are unresurrected Eurydices sleeping quietly above the Lethe of forgetfulness; but Lethe is overflowing its banks and will drown us if we do not hear Orpheus' summoning song.

Orpheus is summoning his Eurydice.

Sacred Colors[1]

"God is light, and in him is no darkness at all."[2] Light differs from color by the fullness of colors contained in it. Color is light that in one respect or another is limited by darkness. From this we get the phenomenality of color. God appears to us as: (1) an absolute being; (2) an infinite being.

The absolute is above light. The infinite can be symbolized by the infinity of colors contained in a ray of white light. That is why "God is light, and in him is no darkness at all." "I beheld," says the prophet Daniel, "that the thrones were set in place, and the Ancient of days did sit, whose garment was white as snow."[3] We, who are beings created in the image and likeness of God, are, in the deepest foundation of our being, turned toward the light. That is why the definitive oppositeness to divinity is *conditionally* revealed to us by the limitation of light to the point of its complete disappearance. If white light is the symbol of the incarnate fullness of being, black light is the symbol of non-being or chaos. Black light phenomenally determines evil as the principle which destroys the fullness of being and makes the latter illusory. The incarnation of non-being in being, making the latter illusory, is symbolized by gray light. And since gray light is produced by the addition of black light to white light, evil can plausibly be defined as mediocre averageness and dubiousness. By defining the devil as a fidgety gray grifter with sniffles and the tail of a Great Dane, Merezhkovsky provided us with a firm basis for a theosophy of colors; unfortunately, though he opened a door leading to further conclusions, he did not make any. From the color gray we can apprehend the real action of evil. Such action consists in essentializing a relation without things that are related; such a relation is a zero, a machine created out of swirls of dust and ashes and whirling without rhyme or reason.

1. First published in the magazine *Mir iskusstva*, 1904, no. 5.
2. 1 John 1:5.
3. Daniel 7:9. KJV slightly altered.

Here is the logic of such mediocre averageness: Let us assume the existence of something non-relative; this non-relative thing is detected by a special type of measurement which we call depthwise, whereas its opposite is called planar. When for the measurement of objects we define three coordinate axes, it depends on us to call one of these three axes the measurement of depth, whereas the axes lying in the perpendicular plane are planar measurements of width and length. Or conversely: we can call the measurement of depth the measurement of width. The choice of the coordinate axes depends on us. If that which is non-relative is deeply comparable with that which is relative, our choice of depth and planarity will always be relative. We resemble the intersection point of the coordinate axes. We are the origin of the coordinates. That is why our choice of reference system according to lines of depth, width, and length is arbitrary. Such logic flattens all depth, tearing everything away and carrying it off—though it does not carry it anywhere, exactly like Kant's noumenon, which limits the illusory reality but is itself non-existent. The world turns out to be an unnecessary picture where all the people are running and have distorted, greenish faces, covered by smoke from factory smoke stacks; they're running and jumping unnecessarily onto trams, just like in cities. One would think that the only real place to run would be—into oneself. But "I"—the only salvation—turns out to be a black abyss into which the dust-eddies swirl, forming grotesque and all-too familiar pictures. And then you feel yourself eternally falling down with all the phantasms, a zero with all the other zeros. But you don't fall down to the bottom, because there's no place to fall down to, when everyone's flying uniformly and decreasing uniformly—so that the world's approaching zero and already equals zero, and the tram keeps meandering along, chased by those poverty-enveloped zeros wearing their hats and caps. You want to shout: "Wake up! This is all absurd!" But shouting would attract a crowd of idlers and perhaps a policeman. The absurdity grows, taking revenge for one's attempt to wake up. You remember Nietzsche: "The desert is growing: woe unto him who contains deserts"[4]—and something disgusting grips the heart. It's the devil—the gray dust, settling on everything.

4. From *Thus Spoke Zarathustra*.

The gray light-extinguishing haze will start to dissipate only when the soul emits a cry of despair. This cry will rip apart the phantasmagoria. "And in that day they shall roar against them like the roaring of the sea: and if one look unto the land, behold darkness and sorrow, and the light is darkened in the heavens thereof."[5] This constitutes an illusion of unexpectedness which appears to reveal the abyss at our feet. He who says this is a real abyss will take relation for essence. Almost all of our contemporary connoisseurs of contemplation in the art of all kinds of abysses are at this stage. It should be remembered that there is as yet no abyss here. What we have is an optical illusion. A cloud of dust has extinguished the lantern in our hands, shutting off the eternal light by an opaque wall. This is a black wall of dust which at first sight appears to be a chasm, just as an unlit closet can appear to be an infinite black universe when darkness, not allowing one to see its limits, blinds one's eyes. One should not be afraid of this rebellious chaos. It should be remembered that it is a veil, a temptation that must be overcome. One must step into the darkness before one can step out of it.

The first shining that cuts through the darkness is tinted with a sinister yellow-brown coating of dust. This sinister gleam is familiar to all awakening sleepers who find themselves in the region between dream and reality. Woe unto him who is not able to dissipate this sinister gleam by overcoming chaos. He will fall, crushed by the phantasm. Lermontov, who was never able to decipher the pathways indicated in his dreams, always broke off his profound insights:

> From my days of childhood
> An unearthly flame has burned in me.
> But fate has ordained that
> It fade in silent futility.[6]

The horror of unfulfilled insights hung over him like an executioner's axe:

> I view the future with fear

5. Isaiah 5:30.
6. From Lermontov's poem "Fragment" (1830).

And the past with anguish,
And like a criminal before his execution,
I seek around me a kindred soul.[7]

And the sunset, in which Lermontov himself saw a sacred smile, shines like a burning flame:

I silently admire the fiery strip
Of sunset outside my window.
Perhaps tomorrow it will gleam above me
Like a cold lifeless corpse.[8]

Lermontov was fated to misunderstand the nature of the mood that tormented him, a mood that could appear (O horror!) to be a pose, or good-natured pessimism, or an instance of the woe of the world, or "poetic" sorrow, whereas all of this actually bore the stamp of sacred prophetic anguish.

But such is the fate of "eyes opening from sleep." They are equally far from dream and from victory:

A fiery tear rolls down my cheek
But it comes not from the heart.
The things stored in my life-deceived heart
Will die in my heart[9]

because

Amid the noise of the world
The word born
From flame and light
Will find no response.[10]

As in a camera obscura the destinies of exceptional individuals

7. From an 1837 poem by Lermontov.
8. From Lermontov's poem "Death" (1830).
9. From Lermontov's poem "Romance" (1831).
10. From an 1840 poem by Lermontov.

reflect the destinies of entire epochs and finally the destinies of universal history. Such individuals tend to become actors who act out our future tragedies—first as actors and then perhaps as the originators of events. If you put on a mask, it grows into your face. Such individuals tend to be points of the application and intersection of universal historical forces. They are windows through which the wind of the future blows on us.

Lermontov was such an individual. In his destiny we recognize destinies that threaten all of us. The executioner's axe that hangs over him threatens all of us.

> Why worry about the fate of the decrepit world?
> The axe hangs over your head
> And it seems that only I can see it.[11]

The horror provoked by the decrepit world over which the axe hangs reminds one of the Gospel's words about the last days when there will be "great tribulation, such as was not since the beginning of the world."[12] A step further and the figure of the coming Avenger must rise before Lermontov, and he does rise:

> The year will come. Russia's black year
> When plague from stinking corpses
> Will roam amid the sorrowing villages
> And fire will color the rivers' waves...
> On that day a man of power will come
> And he will be harsh and horrible.[13]

Here he is echoed by our contemporary poets and prose writers: "The end is near, soon the unexpected will appear."[14] "I envision: a great calamity is near at hand/But as yet no one senses its nearness..."[15]

11. From an 1839 poem by Lermontov.
12. Matthew 24:21.
13. From Lermontov's poem "Prophecy" (1830).
14. From a poem by Vladimir Solovyov.
15. From A.A. Golenishchev-Kutuzov's poem "1 January 1902."

In all of Dostoevsky's novels we encounter "filthy" taverns. It is in such taverns that his principal heroes carry on their most important, abstract, and terrifying conversations about the final destiny of Russian and universal history. And you feel that it is precisely the vulgarity of this Smerdyakov-like setting that imparts to these conversations their threatening and sinister apocalyptic coloration, like the sky before a lightning strike.[16]

A ray of eternal life imbues this seemingly inoffensive vulgar grayness with what constitutes its true and horrible coloration. After overcoming this stage, we come to another trial: everything is permeated with a fiery red shining. From physics we know that it is a property of white light to turn red when passing through a dusty nontransparent medium of a particular thickness and density. Thus, the sensation of red is produced by the relation of the white light to the gray medium. The relative and illusory character of the color red is a fact discovered by theosophy. Here the enemy is revealed to us in his final accessible essence—in the red shining of the fire of hell. It should be remembered that this is the final limit of relativity—the phantasm of a phantasm, who is capable, however, of becoming realer than real by taking on the appearance of a serpent: "And there appeared a great red dragon, having seven heads and ten horns, and seven crowns upon his heads. And his tail drew the third part of the stars of heaven, and did cast them to the earth."[17]

This is the phantasmagoric Haze: it is produced by particles of dust that have settled on man and is only an optical illusion. Love at this stage is tinted by the fiery color of all-devouring passion; it is full of dark bewitchments and an evil earthy fire:

> Alone, I come to you,
> Bewitched by fires of love.
> In your conjuring do not call me:
> I myself have long been conjuring
> The bewitchment-enchained days,

16. Here Bely paraphrases a line from Merezhkovsky's book *L. Tolstoy and Dostoevsky*.

17. Rev. 12:3–4.

I coddle the years—only do not call me.
When will the fires fade
Of this bewitched dark love?[18]

Such a love is capable of showing us the image of her about whom Revelation speaks: "and I saw a woman sit upon a scarlet coloured beast. . . . And upon her forehead was a name written, MYSTERY, BABYLON THE GREAT, THE MOTHER OF HARLOTS AND ABOMINATIONS OF THE EARTH."[19]

Here one cannot remain. Here one will be consumed by fire. One must go forward. Also the words of the Apostle Peter clearly tell us that this is a trial: "Beloved, think it not strange concerning the fiery trial which is to try you, as though some strange thing happened unto you: But rejoice, inasmuch as ye are partakers of Christ's sufferings; that, when his glory shall be revealed, ye may be glad also with exceeding joy."[20] In Isaiah we read: "though your sins be as scarlet, they shall be as white as snow; though they be red like crimson, they shall be as wool."[21] And Merezhkovsky writes: "But in this flame, in this fire which must consume the world, there remains the freshness of the unfading lilies of Galilee. What mystery is contained in these fragrant white lilies, in the fragrance of the resurrected Flesh that is as white as a lily!"[22] It is within our will to extinguish the fire with our own blood and to transform it into a scarlet dawn of suffering. Otherwise we will be consumed in the fire and the wind will swirl our gray ashes and sculpt phantasms out of them. Prayer unto a sweat of blood will sustain us in these hours of burning and annihilate the bewitchment of the red horrors. Only by prayer could Daniel extinguish the burning of the "fiery furnace."

"And he shewed me Joshua the high priest standing before the angel of the Lord, and Satan standing at his right hand to resist him. And the Lord said unto Satan, The Lord rebuke thee, O Satan; even the Lord

18. A 1901 poem by Alexander Blok.
19. Rev. 17:3–5.
20. 1 Peter 4:12–13.
21. Is. 1:18.
22. From *L. Tolstoy and Dostoevsky*.

that hath chosen Jerusalem rebuke thee: is not this a brand plucked out of the fire?"[23] Here the Savior is called "a brand plucked out of the fire?" Christ was incarnated into the center of the struggle and horror and He descended into hell, into the red, in order to overcome the struggle and thus lay free the path for all men.

In the color red are concentrated the horror of fire and the thorns of suffering. This allows us to make sense of the theosophical duality of red. Is it not by virtue of the stage of burning preceding suffering that the Bogomils regard Sataniil as Christ's older brother? Also, is this not why the Manicheans recognize two Creator Gods, a good one and an evil one? But none of this can overcome the abyss between good and evil: Christ will remain in opposition to Satan, as in the prophet Zechariah's vision.

It is not by accident that blood made Him scarlet. It is not by accident that He was clothed in a scarlet robe: *This cup is the new testament* in His blood which He shed for us. It is not by accident that He felt horror and anguish when He cast His sorrowing gaze upon His slumbering disciples: "My soul is exceeding sorrowful, even unto death".... And His sweat of blood moistened the earth. "And they stripped him, and put on Him a scarlet robe. And when they had platted a crown of thorns, they put it upon His head".... At the third hour they crucified Him. "Now from the sixth hour there was darkness over all the land unto the ninth hour. And about the ninth hour Jesus cried with a loud voice, saying, Eli, Eli, lama sabachthani? that is to say, My God, my God, why hast thou forsaken me?" The cross erected at Golgotha separates forever the horror from the joy of the second coming, when He will come with his heavenly armies, "clothed in fine linen, *white* and clean."

The cross erected at Golgotha, all covered with drops of blood; and the crown of fragrant, mystical roses, incorruptible and white! The first centuries of Christianity were rendered scarlet by blood. The peaks of Christianity are as white as snow. The historical evolution of the church is a process of *the whitening of robes by the blood of the Lamb.* Our church, which is not yet victorious but which has already foretasted the sweetness of victory, has all the shades of rosy dawn-like

23. Zech. 3:1–2. The Russian Bible has Iisus (Jesus) for Joshua.

dreaminess. The rose color unites red with white. If we compare the theosophical definition of the color red as the relativity of the struggle between God and the devil with the rose color in which the white light of human divinization is dominant, we will find that the following stage of psychical experience has a rosy tint.

As we approach the absolute, we gain knowledge of ideas. Knowledge of an idea is life-giving. In art, ideas are a source of delight. When they are transformed into symbols which lead us to goals, art touches religion. Ideas are then doubly life-giving. Ascent to the higher spheres of being requires inner knowledge of the paths. Our true guide is prayer. Prayer clarifies the dim glass through which we see. The blinding gleam of the ideal after tears have been shed. Prayer is the condition that transmutes sorrow into joy. Rapture is the rejoicing in ideas. Prayer irresistibly brings ideas into the soul. In prayer, the peaks of art merge with mysticism. The union of mysticism with art is theurgy.

Theurgy transforms our relation to ideas. Ideas are a manifestation of divine principles. In the religion of Zoroaster, ideas are identified with the nine angelic principles. In Christianity there are nine degrees in the angelic hierarchy. In art, ideas are passive. In religion, they exert influence. In art the contemplation of ideas frees one from suffering. Theurgic creativeness enables one to participate in love. We begin to love a phenomenon when we see its idea. We begin to love the world with an ideal love. According to Schopenhauer, feelings are actions of the will. Love is the deepest feeling, the deepest action of the will. "And though I bestow all my goods to feed the poor, and though I give my body to be burned, and have not love, it profiteth me nothing."[24] That is what Paul said. The manifestations of love are diverse. The core of love is often obscured. We often lose touch with its true roots.

If the activity of love must be organized by reason, the question of the degree of the influence of reason on feeling makes the definition of love a philosophical problem. But harmony between reason and feeling is not achieved by compromises between the two. According to Kant, the direct influence of feeling on reason is a source of error. By overcoming reason and feeling through their union, we expand the

24. 1 Cor. 13:3. KJV slightly altered.

forms of knowledge to their greatest generality. Wisdom is the broadest degree of knowledge. The domain of its application is symbolism. Here, all love is transfigurative and symbolic. Symbolic love transposes the point of its application into Eternity. The incarnation of eternity is theurgy. In its essence, love is theurgic, and it is therefore mystical. The organization of love is religious.

If true love consists in unorganized feeling, a new series of questions arises: What is the relation of love to morality, to right, and to law? Some sociologists say that love is an assessment of interests. According to Solovyov, right is the historically shifting definition of the compulsory equilibrium of two moral interests—individual freedom and the common good. Right is reduced to morality. Meanwhile, law, this obligatory organization of right, is subordinate to grace. Grace is a manifestation of divine love. Love, a ray of light from the essence, is outside of right, morality, and law, and must not abolish any of the three. Its essential features here are universality and constancy—that is to say, Eternity. Eternity is made incarnate in theurgy. That is why the direct feeling of love must contain a religious element. Love is ideal. Ideas can be generic or specific. The ideas of the world and of humanity are the most universal. In the visible world, man constitutes the highest degree of objectification that is accessible to our observation. Man contains the essence of the world process. The ideas of the world and of humanity coincide conditionally for us. The idea of the world can be called the soul of the world. According to Solovyov, the soul of the world, Sophia, is the perfect humanity eternally contained in Christ's divine being. Here the mystical essence of the church is conjoined with the image of the eternal feminine, the bride of the Lamb. Here we find the Alpha and the Omega of true love. The relation of Christ to the church, that of bridegroom to bride, is a profoundly cosmic symbol. The light of this symbol reveals all real love. All love is a symbol of this symbol. At its peak intensity, every symbol reveals the image of the Bridegroom and the Bride. The trumpet resounds invitingly from the New Jerusalem. Every symbol has its peak when it is about last things, the end of all. The definitive essence of the last symbol will be revealed when "the new heaven and new earth" are revealed. The Revelation of John ends with the voice of the bride: "Come." The peaks of all the forms of love, conjoined by a common symbol, prepare us for Eternity. What begins here, will end there.

The ray of light from religious love descends on marriage. According to Solovyov, marriage constitutes an image that is sanctified by the word of God and symbolizes the union of Christ with the Church. "The chief significance of marriage lies in the pathos of love. The male sees his natural complement—the woman—not as an object of external observation; rather, he sees her idea, what she is primordially called to be—he sees her the way God has from all eternity seen her and as she must finally become.... She is affirmed as a goal in herself, as a being capable of being *deified*."[25] Until marriage becomes perfect, the succession of generations must fulfill this task.

"A yearning for creative force, an arrow and aspiration toward the superman: Tell me, brother, is that the nature of your aspiration toward marriage?"[26]

The gradual actualization of marriage is a universal historical task. The meaning of this actualization can only be mystical. Any other attitude toward marriage is only formal in character. That type of attitude is a source of unfulfilled hopes.

"I may love someone, but love does not adorn my life," writes Lermontov.[27] Here we find the closest possible approach to the essence of the matter. Disenchantment or even satiation with love is a source of eternal seeking. Eternal love—that is the dawn at the end of the long night.

Nothing will ever bring us close again.
Nothing will bring me peace.
And my heart sometimes whispers to me:
I cannot love another.[28]

Without the crown of suffering the eternal starriness of love will never shine. Only when sharp thorns tear apart the suffering brow and

25. Inexact quotation from Solovyov's *Justification of the Good*.
26. From *Thus Spoke Zarathustra*.
27. From an 1831 poem.
28. Inexact quotation from an 1830 poem by Lermontov.

the cast-off crown of red stars illumines the sky with roses—only then will the starry orgiastic flow burst through the dam. Memory will free the dear image of all finite and accidental features and deepen it into a symbol. And the soul will say:

I cannot love another.

"No, it is not you I love so fervently," says Lermontov. But, then, whom does he love? Whom?

I love my dream's creation
Who has eyes full of azure fire.[29]

That's whom Lermontov loves.

If Lermontov were fully conscious of the interaction between the real creation of his dream with "eyes full of azure fire" and its symbol into which his beloved is transformed, he would be able to cross the gulf separating his earthly love from his eternal one.

Marriage and romantic love acquire the appropriate coloration only when they become symbols of youthful, not yet attained, superhuman relations.

"As the lily among thorns, so is my love among the daughters." That is what the Bridegroom tells the Church, his Bride, in the Song of Songs.

"As the apple tree among the trees of the wood, so is my beloved among the youths."[30] That is the Bride's answer to her Bridegroom.

The temptations threatening us have dissipated, and the caressing dawn gleams like rosy amber. Dawn's pale pearls smile us; and the morning stars, the sky's eternal diamonds, glisten. The bloody crown of thorns is thrown at our feet. Somewhere below burns "the cruel flame of the earthly fire" (as Solovyov says in one of his poems); it burns to an end, coiled into crimson rings—a defeated red dragon, crawling away into timelessness. And farther below, somewhere in the misty abysses, one hears the hollow rumbling of the receding chaos.

29. From an 1840 poem by Lermontov.

30. Song of Solomon 2:2–3. KJV slightly altered.

Until the victory is complete, a sudden swirl of dust, risen from the abysses, can still darken the light. The universal fire will then burn the spaces again; the voice of the bride will break off again; and the great whore upon the scarlet beast will hurtle again and again into the rebellious chaos. The thorns will pierce the brow again.

But the sight of the retreating storms and the dawn caress meekly calm the poor heart.

The image of the mystical church at the boundaries of times and spaces. The spaces melt. The beginning of the times merges with their end. A circle of time is formed—"the ring of rings, the ring of return." The sun will gleam from there. And She will manifest Her image, but a voice emanates from timelessness: "Surely I come quickly."[31]

Christ, Eternity incarnate, is our day full of time. Symbolism is ending; incarnation is beginning. We must make Christ incarnate, just as He made Himself incarnate. Real with a second reality is our love for Christ. "Verily, verily, I say unto you . . . I am that bread of Life. . . . He that eateth My Flesh and drinketh My Blood, dwelleth in Me, and I in him."[32] This is the incarnation or theurgy whereby we, children, nurture the hope of becoming as He is. And even as in transfiguration we know Him by love, so He is made incarnate in every transfigured love. Nietzsche's "day of the great midday," the day when the superman is to come, was and will be again, returning for the second time. "A little while, and ye shall not see me: and again, a little while, and ye shall see me . . . and your heart shall rejoice, and your joy no man taketh from you. . . . These things I have spoken unto you, that in me ye might have peace. In the world ye shall have tribulation: but be of good cheer; I have overcome the world."[33] "But this I say, brethren, the time is short: it remaineth, that both they that have wives be as though they had none; And they that weep, as though they wept not . . . for the image of this world passeth away."[34]

To pass through the modes of "this world," to go away to a place where all are mad in Christ—that is our path. It is not by chance that

31. Rev. 22:20.

32. John 6:47–48, 56. The capitalization is Bely's.

33. John 16:19–33.

34. 1 Cor. 7:29–31. KJV slightly altered.

Maeterlinck speaks of the awakening of the soul. We are at a crossroads and do not yet know which road to take. The end of the modes of perception leads to different modes. This world arises in modes of time and space. For our abiding consciousness the alteration of these modes will erase the image of "this world." A new earth and a new heaven will then appear. This will be the end of this world. The infinite line of causality unfolded in time will, when time is abolished, turn into a point. That which is at the beginning and that which is at the end are one. "I am Alpha and Omega, the beginning and the ending, saith the Lord, who is, and which was, and which is to come, the Almighty."[35] A man who goes outside of time will say with Christ: "now I am no more in the world, but these are in the world, and I come to Thee, Holy Father. . . ."[36] If we look at this man, his azure-clear gaze will reveal nothing. Now we look at each other from two different worlds. When the world ends, there will be fullness of affirmations, finality of images. And conversely: in periods of the soul's awakening, the images arising before us will assume their final forms. The soul has awakened, and there is again talk of the end. We do not know if our crossroads will be the beginning of the end or only its prefiguring. But in the first snowflakes fluttering above us, we have read sacred portents. In the voice of the first blizzard, we have heard the joyous call: "It returns; it returns again." Often, finding ourselves in solitary byways late at night, we have stopped before the crimson light of a lamp of veneration, praying that our whole life be illuminated by such crimson light. A crimson tremor on the dusty silver snow, a clear dark-blue sky with gold. . . . And the blizzard's sorrowfully dear fairy-tales rush onward and someone's voice resounds from timelessness: "but I will see you again, and your heart shall rejoice, and your joy no man taketh from you. . . . And in that day ye shall ask me nothing."[37] The finality of Christianity, the New Testament nature of the thought of the end, the unexpected lightness and joy which are invariably contained in this thought—this is the light that has descended into our soul. Where does this come from? And why?

35. Rev. 1:8. KJV slightly altered.

36. John 17:11.

37. John 16:22–23.

When the dust scatters and the air's whiteness begins to glisten, suddenly we will see the heavenly blue. And in the bright white of the day we will learn to recognize our joy by gazing at the sorrowfully joyful clear azure sky. The white glow looks blue on the colorless background of the cosmic abysses. This is the optical law that is always in effect when whiteness is underlaid with a colorless abyss. And when we gaze into the azure, we see that the impossible appearance of the cosmic abysses is covered with a white veil of air. Only the most penetrating gaze will detect the abyss opening up in the transparent ocean of white air and see it as the background lying beneath this ocean, as a bottom, a bottomless bottom. The union of the cosmic abyss, situated in a timeless and conditionless place, with the white transparence of air symbolizing ideal humanity—this union is revealed to us in the unifying color of the sky, this symbol of divine-humanity, of biunity. Christ says: "he that hath seen Me hath seen the Father. . . . I am in the Father, and the Father in Me. . . ."[38] A whiteness of air veiling the comic abyss—that is what the sky is. Confucius says: "He who knows the nature of things and his own nature, knows what the sky is, for it is nothing else but the inner essence."

Using color symbols, we are able to reconstruct the image of the one who has overcome the world. This image may be dim, but we believe that the mist around it will be dissipated. His face must be as white as snow. His eyes, two apertures into heaven, are sky-blue and amazingly bottomless. His thick golden locks are like flowing mead—the rapture of the saints when they think of heaven. But the sorrow of the righteous when they think of the world is like a wax film covering His face. His lips are bloody crimson, like the crimson that weaves a line of flowers into a circle and will destroy the world by fire. His lips are a crimson fire. Here and there we are able to detect on our neighbors' faces one trait or another of holiness. Bottomless azure eyes will amaze us and we will stand gazing into them as if they were abysses; or the snowy tint of a brow will remind us of a cloud covering the azure. Eternity will shine from a face that is as pure as a child's. It will shine and fade and these sorrowful children will not learn *what name is*

38. John 14:9, 11.

inscribed on their brows. Knowing glimmers of Eternity, we believe that truth will not abandon us, that it is with us. Love is also with us. Loving, we will overcome. Radiance is also with us. O if, resplendent with light, we could ascend! Peace is also with us. And happiness is with us.

Tolstoy[1]

Leo Tolstoy was the most extraordinary phenomenon of Russian life in the 19th century. Pushkin and Gogol were greater artistic geniuses. There might even have been people more extraordinary than Tolstoy, geniuses of life, but the names of such people are often hidden from us; if they existed, their secret accomplishments vanished together with them. There were also men of social and political action around whom coalesced movements that were perhaps more significant. But the mission of the artistic genius is to enchant us with the depth of the reality his works reflect, though he himself often does not know how to interpret and give meaning to this reflected depth of reality. A kind of mediumism develops in the artistic genius; this kind of genius is highly receptive, and the greatest geniuses sometimes astonish us with an extraordinary purely feminine sensitivity, while lacking the masculine ability to actualize the beauty they have seen. Moreover, what they have really seen and experienced in their souls sharply contradicts what they have really seen and experienced in life. In its creative growth human genius is squeezed between art and life: we see countless examples of artistic geniuses with crippled lives. Furthermore, at the deepest basis of artistic creativity lies the need to understand this creativity as an activity directed at the transfiguration of reality; at the deepest basis of the attention we devote to artistic geniuses lies the hope, explicit or implicit, that their art could solve the enigma of our being and that with harmony and a measure of beauty it could alleviate the immense disharmony of our life, which our knowledge allows us to analyze but which we cannot fully understand. And we listen to a genius as if we know that the sources of artistic creativity and those of the creativity of life are one and the same, all the while forgetting that, despite all their qualitative homogeneity, there is a quantitative inequality between the creative intensity of an artist of the word and that

1. This is part III of Bely's essay "The Tragedy of Creativity: Dostoevsky and Tolstoy," Moscow, 1911.

of an artist of life. The pathways of the great lights of life start where the special pathways of art as technique end, whereas art without technique is form without form, i.e., an absurdity. Francis of Assisi starts where Dante ends, but when Francis writes poetry, he loses his authentic meaning for us: that which constitutes the center for the creator of art (e.g., verbal expression, colors, notes) is the periphery for the creator of life; and conversely: that which lies at the center for the creator of life (e.g., the embodiment in one 's acts of the depth of experience) is often a means of expression in form (e.g., in words, in rhythm, in colors) for the creator of art.

We can conceive of a life of genius taking place entirely in muteness, but we refuse to believe that there could be poet of genius who has not written a single line of genius, just as we cannot conceive of a creator of life who lacks a personal life. But however great may be the quantitative distance separating Francis and Dante, qualitatively the souls of both consist of the same substance of creativity. And though the spheres of these two types of creativity may not coincide at all, the peripheries of the spheres touch at least at one point; and this tangential point determines our secret aspiration to seek beauty in the life of the artist of genius or to see a life of genius revealed in words of genius. The existence of this point makes it possible to resolve the tragedy of life in artistic creativity and, conversely, to resolve the tragedy of creativity in life. I even assert that this theoretically possible point determines and conditions the very meaning of the life of genus as life told to others or the meaning of words of genius as really experienced words. For this reason our aspiration to read the creativity of life in the creativity of words or to demand words from creative life is an authentic one. But we are forgetting that this possibility is the rarest of coincidences; it is, so to speak, genius of the second order, and when it is revealed to us, the very direction of culture changes: in essence, we desire to see Confucius, Muhammad, or Buddha in the artistic genius. But we are cruelly deceived; the task of the incarnated artistic genius is a new one: he must find the point uniting the word and the flesh of reality; he must find the word in the gestures of his own life and transform the gesture itself into a beautifully sung song.

But in the other case too we encounter exactly the same thing. Life experienced in a manner of genius often turns out to be a mute life; an experience of genius can have an untalented verbal expression. Depth and acuteness of experience are known even by untalented poets, whose verses are suitable only for the trash bin. Furthermore, deep inner life acutely feels the disharmony between the experiences usually expressed by words and the words themselves. When we say "I love you," how many different nuances these words contain! Enriched by inner life, we see that words give only a pale reflection of our riches; the genius in us is manifested only in the fact that it drinks from the "sources of life" without any possibility of locking these sources in a marble encasement of verbal form; but without this encasement in words the sources of life are polluted. Here Tyutchev is right:

> Excavating them, you'll only muddy the sources.
> Drink from them and keep silent.[2]

Here "the thought when uttered" is only a lie. Deepening of inner life begins with the great experience of "silence." It is not by chance that different schools of experience speak so explicitly of silence: for Ruysbroeck as well as for Maeterlinck, for the eastern school of the Church as well as for Hindu philosophy, silence is the beginning of that path of personal perfection that afterwards leads to preaching. The range of silence varies too; for some the growth of the inner life is always confined within silence, and that is why the teachings of the geniuses of life who have graduated from the school of silence are sometimes so meager, colorless, and virtually contentless; and sometimes we utterly fail to notice those who see much more clearly than we the meaning of life. The path of both types of genius traverses in the same way the glistening magnificence of colors and images; but whereas an artist of words develops in himself a special ability to convey his experiences by means of style, rhythm, the shaping of words, and various techniques of representation and thus stops to refine every image, an artist of life, not stopping, hurries on in silence, advancing farther and farther. The words of the first type of genius run in advance of him; the words of the second type of genius lag far behind him. But for both types there comes a moment when word encounters

2. See note 8 on p. 29.

silence; this is a fateful moment in the life of geniuses: the genius enters into war with himself; words begin to demand life and life begins to demand words; verbal creativity becomes cognizant of its true goal: to become a creativity of life, but this can be achieved only if one has authentic life within oneself. Here the artist of words realizes that the whole technical side of his creativity is a burden which obstructs the movement of creatively experienced life; And, conversely, the artist of life realizes that the treasures of his experience are the property of all mankind; he seeks the possibility of renouncing these riches for himself and transmitting them to all mankind, for he can think of himself only as being connected with the whole world; and then he has recourse to words. This is the moment when the great writer becomes silent and the great man of silence begins to speak. The words of the first fade, become stricter and dryer, or even dry up completely, whereas the silence of the second is exploded by words that shake the world. At that point people often stop understanding an artist and become astonished by his conduct, whereas crowds gather around the man of silence. The first is threatened by self-isolation, the second by self-betrayal.

The man of genius has a dark point that those around him cannot understand: he is called to overcome himself as a genius in the name of a higher order of genius which most people cannot understand; a mountain at the bottom of which people happily reside turns all of a sudden into an active volcano; that which previously had enchanted, begins to horrify people. This dark point is actually the peak of genius; it is an attempt to fuse words about life with a life which cannot be described in ordinary words; muteness begins to speak; words become symbols. Not all men of genius rise to the peak of their genius. Some perish just before reaching the peak; think of Nietzsche's suffering or of Gogol's torments or of Dostoevsky's epileptic fits.

Not too long ago Leo Tolstoy stood on this peak before the face of the universe. In the first half of his life his artistic genius compelled him to say what very few had said before him, and he said it in a way that very few could say it. But his life-wisdom extinguished his former artistic genius; in the second half of his life he no longer said what he had said in *War and Peace* and *Anna Karenina*. He no longer spoke *that* way; he kept *silent*. And of course the writings of the second half of his life did not express the essence of what he kept silent about. I will not dispute many of Tolstoy's followers who assert the philosophical depth or ethical heights of his *penultimate* words. All that is true; but his artistic genius is silent here, and this silence frightens and oppresses us. And, conversely, nothing he said in this later period surpasses what many others had said previously in this vein; he knew what he was doing when he published his *Circle of Reading*.[3] He becomes mute; his words are intentionally clumsy; and when we are enchanted by the beauty of these clumsy, as if stuttering words, what enchants is the titanic power of Tolstoy's silence, resembling the wordless thunder of an imminent volcanic eruption. Tolstoy strove to achieve simplicity; he desired clarity; but this clear simplicity and intentional misunderstanding of all that is most refined by the most refined man of his era signify the extreme lack of simplicity of this man who had simplified himself, the extreme lack of clarity of his childishly clear words. This fusion of what is expressed clearly with the unclarifiable depths of his artistic nature, a nature which had grown silent, constitutes the magnificence of Tolstoy's tragedy—the tragedy of a genius who had overcome his innate human genius in the name of a greater genius, inexpressible and barely comprehensible. In the second half of his life Tolstoy was a man of silence whose teachings barely expressed a thousandth of what was inside him. His clarity and simplicity contained a multitude of figurative meanings; he became a living riddle of human creativity: everyone argued with him and tried to refute Tolstoyism, this pale shadow of the living Tolstoy; everyone tried to prove that Tolstoy was wrong, but nevertheless people were drawn to him. Not his words but he himself was the magnet attracting the whole world. On one side we have the multitude of intellectual, moral, and artistic currents noisily debating one another; on the other side we have Tolstoy, sitting silently in his meadow with his *Circle of Reading*. How incommensurable! The magnetic force emanating for years from Yasnaya Polyana[4] and pushing aside other intellectual and moral currents consisted not in Tolstoy's words or explicit acts but in his silence, a silence eloquently expressed

3. A compilation of what Tolstoy considered to be wise sayings from many of the world's major religious figures.

4. Tolstoy's estate, where he received many visitors in the second period of his life. Yasnaya Polyana means "clear meadow."

in the fact that as his third work of genius he regarded the notorious *Circle of Reading*, a selection of sayings from the world's major sages. Was this not a kind of muteness? It was not a muteness of stagnation or death, however; it was the muteness of the final tragic battle, which lasted for years. This battle was what lured and drew people to him; those who saw him during those years in Yasnaya Polyana found him amazing, maddening, frightening, and oppressive. Many people felt his power and received the light that emanated from him, but many were horrified by him. Clearly, he did not want an enlightenment that was achieved too easily; he wanted the final victory, the final enlightenment; and therefore when he spoke of the light, he himself was not yet in the light. The inertia and weight of earth were still present in him. That's how he seemed to me in the faraway years of my childhood when I had occasion to see him. Here I must mention a personal recollection of my meeting with Tolstoy, a meeting I have never forgotten. Once I was playing hide and seek with some other children in Tolstoy's house in Khamovniki; and one of the children had the idea of hiding in Tolstoy's study, so that Aleksandra Lvovna,[5] who was "seeking" us wouldn't be able find anyone. So, we spread out in darkness in Tolstoy's study: some of us lying on the couches, others on the floor, still others beneath his desk, all of us in the most casual poses. Suddenly Tolstoy walked into the study, holding a candle; somberly, he walked to the desk, sat down, and was silent; and we children, exposed by the light, remained lying in the same casual poses in which he had found us. For what seemed like a minute we lay there in *excruciating silence*; finally, as if not noticing our embarrassment, Tolstoy broke the silence by asking someone a question.

Later on, when I no longer had occasion to see Tolstoy and my thoughts of him were painful and confused, that minute of *excruciating silence* which we children experienced in the presence of the great elder always seemed symbolic to me: did we not hear the same excruciating silence behind the clear and loudly declaimed words of Tolstoyism? Did we not hear the same lack of simplicity in the simplicity of the latter? The great elder gathered children together and spoke to them

5. One of Tolstoy's daughters.

clearly and simply, but you couldn't help feeling that, behind all that clarity, something mute and bottomless was looking out at you from Tolstoy: as it got simpler, it became more bottomless until we reached a *clarity of the depths*. So, all of Tolstoy's reasoning of this period seemed to me not a depth or bottom but a glistening surface of water, simplifying objects. It appeared to be so easy to refute him, but here's the strange thing: all refutations of his doctrine just seemed to make it more attractive. It was clear that the important thing was not the doctrine but Tolstoy himself: the artistic genius in Tolstoy deliberately immersed himself in silence and was replaced by a philosopher and preacher. But his preaching spoke not with what it desired to be, not with what is passed itself off as; it spoke not explicitly but secretly—not with words but with silence. It was the mystery of his creativity of life that was silent in Tolstoy. That Tolstoy's life was a life of genius, that Tolstoy himself was a work of art—this we did not know then and could not have known, just as sometimes we do not know other life-experiences of genius hidden from us. We were only sad that the artist of the word in Tolstoy was killing himself, and we couldn't understand why he was doing so. We needed a sign, a gesture without words, but one that spoke more loudly than words. We denied this gesture in Tolstoy. But now it has become clear that the silence of his artistic genius was only a deepening of his genius, the agonizing attainment of the highest and final point: Tolstoy's creative activity, having expressed much in words, spoke even more eloquently by silence, and the words that veiled his silence turned out to be a spontaneous act of ascesis.

Suddenly this silence was ripped apart; the veil of Tolstoyism was ripped apart. The artist of genius turned out to be the creator of genius of his own life during this long period of silence. The word became flesh: the genius of life and the genius of the word united in a higher unity. Yasnaya Polyana truly became "clear," as if illuminated by a lightning flash of the final union. Tolstoy rose, went into the world, and—died. By his departure and death he illuminated with his light the poor fields of Russia. To this point Gogol's terrible "troika"[6] had

6. Image from Gogol's *Dead Souls*.

barreled over these fields, blizzards[7] had raged, grievous grief had roamed: these are the spaces of Russian life where the people, together with Pushkin and Gogol, see demons, the spaces into which the Russian intelligentsia goes to die, the spaces where the Russian administrative bureaucracy in the person of Pobedonostsev[8] keeps track of "undesirable elements." Now, through Tolstoy, all these spaces, at least for a moment, have become "clear meadows." The great Russian artist showed us an ideal of holiness; he built a bridge to the people: religion and areligiosity, silence and words, the creativity of life and artistic creativity, the intelligentsia and the people—all these things merged in the final eloquent gesture of genius of the dying Tolstoy. Other Russian writers were set on a pedestal because they read lectures, preached, suffered. But they died within four walls, alone with themselves, in silence. Tolstoy also read and preached. But the greatest pedestal turned out to be death: he climbed up on this pedestal which is virtually inaccessible to mortals and he fell, in front of everyone, in "clear meadows," where he died. His departure and death were the best preaching, the best work of art, the best act of life. Life, preaching, and creative activity merged in a single gesture, in a single moment. This gesture of genius illuminated by Tolstoy was the same dark point in genius that killed Nietzsche and Gogol and crippled Dostoevsky's life when they approached it. Approach to the final mystery of artistic creation produced an explosion. But only in Tolstoy was this dark point of genius illuminated by a clear and grace-bestowing light. The center of artistic activity suffused by the light of Tolstoy's personality showed us once and for all that this center is the periphery of religious creativity: the end turned out to be the beginning. And Tolstoy's final creative gesture was his first religious gesture, the first ray of the sun of life rising over the Russian land.

Tolstoy's activity redeems to some extent our own inactivity: the light of his final days removes the horror of recent years.[9] Let those

7. Allusion to Pushkin's tale "The Blizzard."

8. Konstantin Pobedonostsev, chief administrator of oppressive laws in late 19th-century Russia.

9. Bely is referring to such events as the disastrous war with Japan, the failed revolution of 1905, and the repressions that followed.

days then be the first days of spring; we must say that in the name of Tolstoy.

Russia is not Petersburg and Moscow. Nor is she Skotoprigon'evsk or the town where Peredonov lived. Nor is she Okurov or Likhov.[10] Russia is Astapovo,[11] surrounded by vast spaces; and these spaces are not "evil"[12] spaces; they are "clear meadows," as radiant as God's day.

10. Bely refers to a number of towns of fiction: Skotoprigon'evsk, where *The Brothers Karamazov* is set; Okurov, where Maksim Gorky's stories *The Town of Okurov* are set; and Likhov, where Bely's own novel *The Silver Dove* is set. Likhov is derived from "likhii" (evil, malevolent). Peredonov is the repulsive protagonist of Fyodor Sologub's novel *The Petty Demon*.

11. Tolstoy died at a railway station near the village of Astapovo.

12. The Russian word is "likhie."

Recollections of Vladimir Solovyov[1]

There are companions of childhood whose names and associations strike the child as somehow extraordinary. His imagination becomes overheated, and simple words and phrases take on a golden fairy-tale quality. And names previously unfamiliar acquire a special radiance.

I was first introduced to Vladimir Solovyov when I was already fairly grown-up, though I had heard of him much earlier.

I don't know who first spoke about him in my presence, or where this happened, but in my early childhood he passed through my imagination like a bright star. He seemed strange and frightening to me—perhaps because as a child who was habitually in the company of grown-ups I listened attentively to their obscure words and abstract debates. And my memory would readily retain unfamiliar names. For some reason the names Weierstrass[2] and Solovyov were particularly unforgettable to me. I seem to remember that one of my father's university colleagues once said: "What a strange man Vladimir Solovyov is." And that a lady replied: "Yes, he's quite enigmatic." And the child's imagination started working. I began to think of Vladimir Solovyov as a wanderer with staff in hand roaming through forests and going from town to town and from village to village. A figure somewhat like Wagner's Wanderer, he could pop up anywhere—in Moscow or in the Arabian desert.[3] He did not often traverse my world of fairy-tale imaginings, but he did traverse it. Where was he going? To Arabia? To

1. First published in the magazine *Russkoye slovo*, 1907, December 2.

2. Karl Weierstrass (1815–1897), eminent German mathematician. The young Bely would have heard the name around the house because his father, Nikolai Bugaev, was a leading Russian mathematician and had studied with Weierstrass in Germany.

3. Allusion to Solovyov's travels in Egypt in 1875, where he had the third of his visions of Sophia as described in his poem *Three Meetings*.

the North? He was like one of those musicians traveling north in the *Drama of Life*[4] who announced the approach of delirium. This was providential: later on, Solovyov became for me the precursor of my delirium of religious seekings.

I remember once the doorbell rang. My father wasn't home. A man entered who, to my eyes, looked thin, tall, black, and bent, with hair falling onto his shoulders, a long black-gray beard, emaciated face, and deep gray eyes. He sat down and appeared good-natured and small, because his legs were long; he sat with knees raised high and laughed with his enormous mouth, while stretching toward me a long, bony, and extremely frail-looking hand. He sat for a while and then disappeared. From a conversation between my mother and father I learned that this was Vladimir Solovyov. He had come on some business, but to me he seemed like one of those fabulous strangers from Hoffmann's tales. The grown-ups said that in the desert he had been taken for a demon.[5] I imagined that when he came that time to visit us, he had just come out of the sandstorms of the Arabian Simoom; and that when he went out the door, he swirled away like a sandstorm, like a blizzard. My imagining became more real than reality for me.

Soon afterwards I saw him again at Professor Storozhenko's.[6] I was again struck by his tormented thought-burned face amid the serene and contented faces that surrounded him. It looked to me as if he were about to place his head on his knees, so high did he raise the knees of his long legs, whereas his torso seemed short. We, children, ran amidst the guests, trying to pin paper tails to the backs of their suit-jackets. We, children, cast glances of fake terror at Solovyov, while this "boogeyman" gazed at us good-naturedly.

And that was how the fairly-tale figure of Vladimir Solovyov flashed past me in my early childhood. Later on, he and I were formally introduced. But the only meeting with him that had fateful and profound meaning for me was our last meeting, not long before his death.

4. Unidentified work.

5. This is described in *Three Meetings*.

6. N.I. Storozhenko, a historian of literature and close friend of Bely's father, was a professor at the University of Moscow.

His enormous, enchanted gray eyes; his bent back; his long, frail-looking hands; his beautiful head with its gray mane; his large mouth, like a gash with a protruding lip; his wrinkles—Solovyov's appearance contained so much that was contradictory and ambiguous! The French have a word, untranslatable into Russian, that perfectly characterizes the impression that Solovyov made on others: The French would say about him: "*Il était bizarre.*" A giant with frail hands, long legs but a short torso, spiritual eyes but a sensual mouth, the words of a prophet but suddenly you see him stretching a long hand toward a tray of cookies that is being carried past: bending over the treats, he scrutinizes every candy and every cookie with a helplessly guilty smile, and his clawlike fingers grab several goodies, while he rocks with gratitude and embarrassment before the servant. Then he turns to talk to someone, forgetting all about the handful of goodies he had selected so painstakingly; he will utter only a single sentence (he never says much), but it will shine like the dawn. A helpless infant with a lion's mane, a wicked demon muddying the conversation with his lethal laughter ("hee-hee")—and suddenly the dawn, the dawn!

Solovyov always lived under the sign of the dawns that shone for him. It was out of the dawn that the mysterious muse of his mystical philosophy appeared (he called her "she"). She first appeared to him when he was a child. She then appeared to him at the British Museum and whispered to him: "Go to Egypt."[7] And the young scholar rushed to Egypt and almost perished in the desert, before he was visited by a vision suffused with "golden azure."[8] And out of the Egyptian deserts was born his gnostic philosophy—his doctrine of the eternal-feminine principle of divinity. His muse became the norm of his theory as well as the norm of his life. It would not be wrong to say that Solovyov transformed the striving toward the dawn into his duty and that he dedicated eight volumes of his works to fulfilling this duty—volumes where a subtle critical analysis alternates with a diffuse unprovable metaphysics and a great depth of mystical experiences. Trying to decode his doctrine, we encounter an enormous erudition as well as a

7. He described this completely real fact in his poem *Three Meetings*. (Bely's note)
8. Quotation from *Three Meetings*.

diabolical polemical skill which he often abused: he fired his critiques as out of a cannon at enemies and friends alike, and even—alas!—at sparrows. But if you try to discover why he spent his whole life attacking, scourging, and making appeals, you'll find nothing but pale and lifeless metaphysical theories beneath all his critiques and polemics. For Solovyov himself this metaphysics was only a veil of modesty covering a mystery known only to him—the dawn voice of his muse. This voice whispered to him: "Go to Egypt." But it also whispered: "Polemicize with Strakhov,[9] for Strakhov represents death." Such was Solovyov's life—everywhere and always to be illuminated by dawn. Dawn took the form of a beautiful muse and lured him. And from the *Hotel d'Angleterre* in Petersburg he rushed to Saimaa,[10] and then to Moscow, to visit N. Ia. Grot,[11] after which Grot nearly became preoccupied with spiritism. And then Solovyov went to Egypt.[12]

I remember the large brown candles that Solovyov brought back from Egypt as a gift for his brother Mikhail. Indeed, it is as if Solovyov went everywhere carrying a large brown Egyptian candle that was invisible for his distinguished and stable friends but that was perhaps visible for certain of his friends who were rumored to be "dark personalities." It was these dark personalities who were the first to proclaim that Solovyov was not a philosopher but a wanderer walking before God.

Stasiulevich[13] would of course not have seen the candle in Solovyov's hands; nor would it have been visible to his idealist friends who were all distinguished professors and addressed Solovyov in the familiar form. They transformed his doctrine into a type of philosophical idealism, and not even in the neo-Kantian sense; for them his philosophy was only a convenient means to counteract positivism, whereas

9. Allusion to Nikolai Strakhov (1828–1896), prominent Russian philosopher and critic.

10. Lake in southeastern Finland which Solovyov liked to visit, and to which he dedicated one of his best poems.

11. Nikolai Grot (1852–1899), Russian idealist philosopher.

12. Allusion to Solovyov's second journey to Egypt, in 1898.

13. Allusion to the prominent liberal intellectual M.M. Stasiulevich, who was very far from believing in mystical experiences.

even if Solovyov had once opposed positivism, this was only in his youth, and afterwards he even, in his own manner, accepted and clarified Comte's positivism.

That's why Solovyov felt himself alone, although he had enough "friends" to convene an entire psychological convention. And from the green table where these "friends" uttered such important speeches that should have been so agreeable to him, he'd flee to the cold torrents of the many-voiced Imatra or to the white bellflowers of Pustyn'ka;[14] or he'd go directly to the "suspicious personalities": to drunken prophets, to holy fools who had made a mess of their lives, to beggars who were friends of his, or to random cab-drivers, giving them all his money. After the philosopher's death, we learned of his strange connections with many of "the wretched of the earth." What is even stranger, however, is that it is to these "wretched" that he perhaps showed his true countenance.

Many readers will consider my words fantastic and say that now that he's dead, one can write anything one pleases about Solovyov. But I'm sure that people close to Solovyov who knew him intimately will agree with me. True, I had occasion to meet him in the circle of professors and to hear about him from his "respected" friends. But I also saw his manuscripts and heard the reading of his intimate letters. Mainly, I learned about him from a highly reliable source: his brother Mikhail, to whom he was very close and into whose home I was received as one of the family.[15] First as a high school student and then as a university student I spent all my free time in the cozy living-room of his brother's home. We carried on endless conversations there, and many of these conversations were devoted, directly or indirectly, to the deceased philosopher. Mikhail Solovyov was a remarkable man: he combined serene stability and erudition with an unconstrained freedom which did not impede anything that was sincere, whatever form this sincerity might

14. Imatra is a waterfall near Lake Saimaa. Pustyn'ka is a country estate (formerly belonging to his friend Count Aleksey Tolstoy) where Solovyov used to stay at times. One of Solovyov's last poems is entitled "Again the White Bellflowers" (July 8, 1900).

15. Bely was best friends with Mikhail's son Sergei, the future poet and biographer of his famous uncle.

take. He was an authority both for his brother and for his brother's "distinguished" friends, as well as for the small group of young seekers who at that time were treated with contempt by the "distinguished" academics. The Solovyov home attracted bold and sincere men who sought their own paths.

Mikhail Solovyov loved in his brother not the author of eight volumes but the new man who had heard the call in the velvet caress of the dawn and in the quiet swishing of the white bellflowers: "How many of them have recently been blooming!"[16] That is why I could not fail to learn to love in Solovyov not only the thinker but also the audacious innovator of life, who hid his new countenance beneath the visor of an unintelligible metaphysics. And I could not fail to look upon Vladimir Solovyov with profound love when I'd meet him in his brother's home sitting at a small cozy table beneath a soft lampshade. And something soft, sad, and dear would bloom in my heart—flower after flower of those that "have recently been blooming," so recently, only seven or eight years ago! And so seven years have passed and holy lamps glimmer over the three unforgettable graves,[17] and Vladimir Solovyov's personality is departing somewhere into the distance, becoming legendary. And all that's left is the sad birches sighing, sighing with the swishing of spring leaves, which will drift down in the fall to be replaced by the snowstorms that will swirl their wild whirlwinds over the quiet graveyard.

Sick and frail-looking, Solovyov came to visit his brother as if from unknown lands. Small, frail-looking, and with a thick mane of unruly hair, he'd sit playing checkers with his brother, interrupting our conversation with a roaring joke or with a remark that would take the ground from under our feet. But most often he'd roar with laughter at the jokes of his little nephew[18] (now a talented poet), whinnying wildly and stamping with his feet on the floor. Sometimes when I'd go to visit the Solovyov home, I'd see in the vestibule a large fur hat like those worn by priests and a large fur coat like those worn by priests, and I knew that Vladimir Solovyov was there. I'd go in and extending a

16. From Solovyov's poem "White Bellflowers" (August 15, 1899).

17. The graves of Vladimir, Mikhail, and Mikhail's wife.

18. Sergei Solovyov.

long, frail hand to me, he'd say, without looking at me: "Did you know you have the same name as B. N. Chicherin?"[19]

Then he'd rapidly move a checker. He'd listen and whinny. Someone would read verses. If he found anything inept or funny in them, he'd emit his thunderously furious "ha-ha-ha," inciting us to say something paradoxical or crazy. Nothing in our conversation could surprise him: with good-natured thunder he'd emit his "Ha-ha-ha! What nonsense!" And in his presence the conversation would always sparkle like champagne. He would judge a conversation not by the weightiness of proofs but by the quality of wit. In his articles and essays he tried to resemble a camel loaded down with antiquated scholasticism, but the infrequent aphorisms he uttered as he was playing checkers were full of freedom, capriciousness, and startling wit. Dropping all intermediary linkages of thought, he spoke in brief aphorisms; he loved it when thought would leap from peak to peak, and he was not bereft of boldness; and whereas his distinguished friends dragged thought from peak to peak of logical deduction as if driving a creaking cart, he performed a series of leaps. And we, young representatives of the so-called decadent poetry, felt that Solovyov was one of us, that he was kindred and close to us in his language and in the psychical temper of his experiences. I always admired the person of Vladimir Solovyov.

I admired him at the table. I also admired him on the street. He'd ride by through whirlwinds of snow wearing his large priestly hat and wrapped in furs. I'd also encounter him in bleak, dark doorways, where he strode, stamping the ground with his galoshes like a priest late for the service. Then he'd disappear. And I'd encounter him again behind a cozy tea-table.

I remember, it was the spring of 1900. Solovyov was at this time very painfully conscious of the disharmony between his entire literary and philosophical activity and his cherished desire to walk before people with a large Egyptian candle. He told his brother that his mission was not to write philosophical books, that everything he had written was only a prologue to his future activity. This was a little after he had

19. Bely (real name: Boris Nikolaevich Bugaev) had the same first name and patronymic as Boris Nikolaevich Chicherin (1828–1904), eminent legal philosopher and historian. [Bely's note: Since childhood I was used to being reminded of this.]

read to us his "End of Universal History."[20] At that reading he and I met in a new way, as if for the first time, but it was also our last meeting. Solovyov died that summer.

I remember, I received a note from O.M. Solovyov.[21] She informed me that Vladimir Solovyov was going to read the "Third Conversation," and she requested that I attend. I arrived. Solovyov was sitting, sad and weary-looking, with that mark of death and terrifying majesty that never left him in his last months: it was as if he had seen what no one else had ever seen and as if he could not find the words to express his knowledge. During those days much anxiety had accumulated in my soul. When I saw him, I wanted to say something to him that people don't say at a tea-table. But I suppressed my urge, and instead spoke to him about Nietzsche, about the connection between the superman and the idea of divine humanity. He didn't say much about Nietzsche, but what he did say was marked by a profound seriousness. He said that Nietzsche's ideas must be regarded as the greatest threat confronting present-day religious culture. However different my view of Nietzsche might have been, I found profoundly gratifying his serious attitude toward the German philosopher at that moment. I understood that Solovyov's famous belittling characterization of Nietzsche as a "superphilologist" had only been a tactic designed to evade the threat Nietzsche posed to Solovyov's yearnings.

But it was time to begin the reading. Suddenly the doorbell rang. Solovyov became agitated: "Can't you just tell her...?" Here he began to rub his forehead and to think of improbable pretexts to get rid of the lady who had dropped in by chance on the evening of the reading, which was supposed to be reserved for family and close friends. At last he began. As he was reading the "Tale about the Antichrist," when he arrived at the words "Elder John rose like a white candle," he rose up from his armchair. Lightning was flashing in the window and Solovyov's face was trembling in a lightning of inspiration. Here I

20. Allusion to a private reading in Mikhail Solovyov's home (which Bely attended) of the third conversation including "A Short Tale about the Antichrist" from Solovyov's *Three Conversations on War, Progress, and the End of Universal History*.

21. Olga Solovyov, Mikhail's wife.

couldn't refrain from saying something that was particularly close to my heart, something I had found in the dialogue of the "Third Conversation." Startled, Solovyov looked at me. And in response to my "timid" remark, incomprehensible to all the others, he said to me: "Yes, yes. That's right." I felt that a special connection had been formed between him and me. Solovyov told me to go home and bring back a manuscript of mine which touched on the subject around which our views had unexpectedly converged. But O.M. Solovyov said: "It's already late." Solovyov and I agreed to meet after the summer. I knew that our meeting would be a significant one. But Solovyov died. And the word unspoken between us became a sign for me, as did his grave, illuminated by the red lamp.

Afterwards, I often visited places where Solovyov had stayed. Not long ago, I saw his beloved white bellflowers after they had been transplanted from Pustyn'ka. Not long ago I had occasion to wear on a rainy day his enormous rain-proof cloak. And in my mind I clearly saw the dear figure in his cloak as he bent over the white bellflowers at dawn—the figure of an eternal wanderer leaving the old earth and entering the *new city*. And, behind him, other dear figures who had departed into eternity were also resurrected.

Apocalypse in Russian Poetry[1]

Panmongolism![2]
I have a presentiment of You.[3]

I

There is no separation. Life is one. The manifestation of the many is only an illusion. Whatever partitions we may put up between the phenomena of the world, these partitions are immaterial and unreal. They are created by the different types of relations of the one to itself. Multiplicity arises as a mediation of unity, as differences in the folds of one fabric, shaped by the one. If you rip the veil from the world, all these factories, people, and plants will disappear; and like a sleeping beauty the world will awake into integral unity—she will shake her pearl-like locks, her face will shine with the dawn and her eyes with azure, her cheeks will be like little snowy clouds, and her lips will glow like fire. The sleeping beauty will rise—and laugh. The black clouds that had shrouded her will be pierced by her beams of light; they will explode with fire and blood; the contours of the dragon will be visible on them, and the defeated red dragon will dissipate in the midst of the pure heavens.

II

It was the spring of 1900. The dark wing of days to come cast a shadow on the present day, and anxious dreams arose in the soul. The unique path was revealed to humankind. The contours of the religion of the future became visible. A breath of the Eternal Feminine touched us.

1. First published in the magazine *Vesy*, 1905, no. 4.
2. Allusion to Vladimir Solovyov's poem "Panmongolism."
3. From Alexander Blok's poem "I have a presentiment of You. The years are passing by" (1901).

Solovyov's reading of his "End of Universal History" struck us like a bolt of lightning.[4] But the great mystic was right. I remember his bottomless staring eyes and the mane of hair flowing over his shoulders; he was ironically calm, pensive, shrouded in a cloud of fire. He expelled his words sharply and distinctly like splashes of lightning, and those splashes pierced the future. Our hearts were captivated by a mysterious sweetness when he comfortably bent over the manuscript his Biblical prophet's countenance; and tableau after tableau rose in the mist which veiled the future. We saw a series of icy peaks, a range of snow-glistening mountains which we had to cross without falling into the chasm below. The smoke of clouds wove its way up the black abysses; the rays of the sun, splashing the clouds with blood, sketched in the smoke the coming countenance of the dragon flaming in its fury.

But from the immortal heights of Platonism and Schellingism Solovyov saw the rosy smile of the World Soul. He understood the sweetness of the Song of Songs as well as the sign of the "Woman clothed in the sun." And then, from his philosophical heights, he came down into this world in order to show people the perils that threatened them and the raptures they did not know. His voice roared through the comfortable rooms, and his long hands feverishly turned page after page. Strong and authoritative, he battled against horror; it was as if he was not turning pages but tearing the mask from the truth concealed by the enemy. Mask after mask flew off; mask after mask disintegrated into misty dust. And the dust caught fire. "The cruel flame of the earthly fire" raged.[5] But "all things, whirling, were vanishing into darkness,"[6] and we sat at the tea-table and listened to his jokes as—after having finished his reading—he bounced his insanely childlike laughter off the walls. But the visions he had summoned remained in all their horror in the golden lightning that kept flashing through the spring windows.

4. Allusion to a private reading in 1900 of the third conversation including "A Short Tale about the Antichrist" from Solovyov's *Three Conversations on War, Progress, and the End of Universal History.*

5. From Solovyov's sophianic poem "All in azure did my empress appear today before me" (1875).

6. From Solovyov's poem "Poor friend, the arduous path has exhausted you" (1887).

I was struck not so much by the "Tale about the Antichrist" as by what the characters in *Three Conversations* said: "For about a year now I've begun to notice—it's hard to define: I'm not sure if it's in the air or in my soul—I've begun to notice a feeling of anxiety, the sense of something sinister." These words echoed something hard to define that I myself had been feeling. I asked Solovyov whether he had consciously emphasized that the anxiety was like a haze surrounding the world. He told me that he had done it consciously. Later the words about the "haze" were confirmed literally when the Martinique volcano erupted[7] and spewed out black dust which covered the earth like a net and produced purple dawns and sunsets. I already understood then that the causes of this net that had covered that world were rooted in the depths of the individual consciousness. But the depths of consciousness are rooted in the universal unity. I already understood then that the haze shrouding our spiritual gaze would fall on Russia, manifesting outwardly all the horrors of global and internecine wars. I awaited outward signs hinting at that which was taking place inside us. I knew: a fireworks of chimeras would explode over humankind.

Reality did not delay in fulfilling my expectations: Merezhkovsky proclaimed the apocalyptic deadness of European life, which was preparing to give birth to the "Coming Boor." Embodying chaos and risen from the depths, a new type appeared—the hooligan. The specter of a Mongol invasion filled people with fear. A whirlwind blew through European humankind, swirling up clouds of dust. The dust-veiled light turned red, as if the world fire had begun. Nietzsche, on the eve of his madness, had already foreseen the universal historical necessity of a world convulsion, sliding like a grimace across the face of humankind. The "world grimace," the mask pulled over the world, had also horrified Solovyov. Merezhkovsky had pointed to the global madness eating away at humankind. Inwardly, the chaos takes the form of madness; outwardly, it manifests itself as the fragmentation of life into an immense number of separate streams. We find the same thing in science: poorly conceived specialization produces a multitude

7. Allusion to the eruption of Mount Pelée on May 8, 1902 which killed 29,000 people.

of engineers and technology experts with a mask of learning on their faces and with a chaotic and unprincipled madness in their hearts. The immoral application of science has engendered the horrors of the present war with Japan, a war which can be viewed as a symbol of the rising chaos. When we read Ludovic Naudeau's brochure, "They Did Not Know,"[8] we learn that all our military operations were an optical illusion. Japan is a mask hiding invisible forces. The problem of defeating our enemy is closely connected with the necessity of altering our consciousness in a way that will enable it to solve the profoundest mystical problems of European humankind.

Solovyov had a profound vision of the global masquerade in which we are participating. The haze that had appeared in the atmosphere after his death[9] has settled somewhat, as if beaten down by rain. The heaven of our profoundest psychical depths has become cleaner. Someone's eternal, serenely azure eyes are shining at us there, even though the dust that had been swirling in the atmosphere has settled on all objects, on all faces, sharply delineating and almost distorting their natural features and producing an unconscious masquerade.

The whirlwind that is blowing in our Russia, swirling up all the dust, must inevitably create the specter of a red terror, a cloud of smoke and fire, since light sets dust afire when it suffuses it. One must remember that the red dragon flying at us from the East is illusory; it is a series of dark clouds, not a reality; and the war does not exist but is only a product of our sick imagination, an external symbol in the battle of the universal soul against the world horror, a symbol of the battle of our souls against the chimeras and hydras of chaos. Futile is our battle against the terrible hydra: however many heads we may cut off, new ones will grow, until we realize that the hydra is imaginary. It is a Mask pulled over reality, and until we realize that the Mask is imaginary, it will continue to grow, composing bloody universal-historical tableaux: the outwardly attacking dragon will unite with the red rooster spreading its wings over the old estates in the heart of Russia, and all will drown

8. In this work, the French journalist Naudeau, an eyewitness, describes the Russian campaign against Japan in 1904.

9. Solovyov died on July 31 (old style), 1900.

in a sea of fire.[10] And its "red laugh"[11] will set fire to the universe. For those blinded with horror, the end of the world is only the global "red laugh" of horror.

Leonid Andreyev is accused of subjectivism: instead of describing the mass movement of troops or presenting a realistic picture of war, he seems to record nightmarish dreams, but that shows how insightful he is about our contemporary events. Here is what the eyewitness Naudeau has to say about the war: "In contemporary war everything is mysterious, scattered, distant, invisible, abstract; it is a battle of gestures, of aerial signaling, of electrical or heliographic communications. . . . If you approach the fighting forces, you will see nothing in front of you. . . . If you approach a cannon, it is hidden behind a fortification and seems to be firing aimlessly and senselessly into space. . . . You are constantly being deceived by phantasmagorias. . . . This war is invisible, amorphous, hidden. . . . Who took Liaoyang? The Japanese army? Yes, of course, it was the Japanese army, but with the help of nightmare. . . . The need for hope, illusion, apathy, fantasy, imaginary things, ignorance of reality—that's what the first campaign consisted of." Solovyov attempted to show us the attractive mask of falsehood that had been pulled over the countenance of Her[12] who is destined to unite the disunited heaven and earth of our soul into an ineffable unity. Only the dawn petals of the eternal rose can assuage the ferocity of the hellish flame licking the world. The Eternal Woman saves us at moments of deathly peril. It is not by chance that the eternally feminine figure of Brunhilde is encircled by a fiery river or that she is guarded by Fafner, a monstrous dragon. Solovyov showed us the mask of madness that has come into the world and he called all those attacked by the specter to go deep into themselves in order to keep from losing their minds. But to go deep into oneself all the way to the eternally feminine sources of the Soul is to manifest Her countenance before all people.

10. The "red rooster" refers to fires started by angry peasants in order to destroy their hated masters' estates.

11. Allusion to Leonid Andreyev's "The Red Laugh" (1904), a nightmarish, apocalyptic tale set against the background of Russia's humiliating defeat in the Russo-Japanese War.

12. Allusion to Sophia, the "Woman clothed in the sun."

This is the origin of the theurgic power of his poetry, where Fet's pantheism and Lermontov's individualism merge with the radiant insights of the Christian gnostics.

After that unforgettable evening I did not see Solovyov again, but much has been revealed to me since then. I did not understand Solovyov's constant apostrophes directed at his Radiant Feminine Friend, but the dawn encircling the horizon tempered my anxiety. I realized that this anxiety was not mine alone, but affected everyone. In those days I realized that the dawn smiles and the azure of the heavenly fires had a global nature. I began to understand that just as in contemporary war all things are mysterious, scattered, remote, invisible, and abstract, it was the same way with the mystical waves that roll over the world to collide in battle: this battle begins not with visible acts but with a battle of gestures, an aerial signaling. Everything begins with sudden mute flashes of lightning. But the flashes grow. Their muteness explodes into thunder. Then in this actualization by lightning the objects surrounding us become symbols; human masks appear. Finally, the masks fall away and before us we see faces burned by the dawn. They are embodied in the world. The icy fetters of the darkness fade. Hearts hear the flight of spring.

III

The goal of poetry is to find the countenance of the muse and to express in this countenance the global unity of universal truth. The goal of religion is to make incarnate this unity. Religion transforms the image of the muse into the integral countenance of Humanity, the countenance of the Woman clothed in the sun. Art is therefore the shortest path to religion; here humanity, having attained knowledge of its essence, is unified by the unity of the Eternal Woman; taken to its end, creativity is directly transformed into religious creativity—into theurgy. By means of marble, paints, and words, art creates the life of the Eternal Woman; religion rips off this veil. One can say that Her smile reposes on every statue made of marble, and conversely that She is the Madonna sculpted in the ages. The primordial chaos, which had formed according to the laws of free necessity, is deified and becomes Her body. If Humanity is the realest all-unity, then populism is the first limitation of Humanity. Here before us we see a path to unity through the free and spontaneous development of the people's powers. The image of the muse must crown the development of national poetry.

The development of Russian poetry from Pushkin to our own day is accompanied by a three-fold change in the original aspect of this poetry. Three veils are ripped off the face of the Russian muse; three perils threaten Her emergence. The first veil is ripped off from Pushkin's muse, the second from Lermontov's muse; the removal of the third veil leads to the appearance of the Eternal Woman.[13] Two directions are clearly marked in Russian poetry. One has its origin in Pushkin, the other in Lermontov. The poet's relation to the one or the other of these directions determines the character of the poetry of Nekrasov, Tyutchev, Fet, Solovyov, Briusov, and finally Blok. These names are implanted deep in our soul: the talent of these poets corresponds to their providential position in the general system of the development of the national art. If a poet is not preoccupied with solving the riddle of Pushkin's or Lermontov's art, he cannot excite us profoundly.

Pushkin represents wholeness. He wholly encompasses the national unity from outside. When he plays his lyre, Russia arises before us with her fields, towns, and history. He *perfectly* conveys the all-human ideal implanted in the depths of the national spirit; that is why his muse can reincarnate herself in diverse forms. Unconsciously, he indicates the deep roots of the Russian soul, extending all the way to universal chaos. But the wholeness represented by Pushkin's muse is not yet ideal wholeness. The countenance of his muse is not yet the revealed image of Russian poetry. She is still invisible behind the blizzard; the chaos of snowstorms still forms a veil around Her. She still "sleeps in an icy grave, bewitched by sleep." Pushkin's wholeness lacks true depth: it must split apart as it seeks the path to the bewitched beauty. Its elements, which had formed for us the picture of national wholeness, must be regrouped into a new unity. This requirement wholly defines the path of the successors of the Pushkin school: their task is to prepare the incorruptible body of the World Soul in the depths of the Russian nationality; only unorganized chaos can form the body of the organizing principle. The Pushkin school must therefore approach the chaos,

13. Solovyov's vision of Sophia.

rip off the veil covering it, and overcome it. Pushkin's successors—Nekrasov and Tyutchev—split apart the whole kernel of his art, deepening parts of the fragmented unity.

The stirring sky of Russian nature sketched by Pushkin is covered by Nekrasov with sorrowful gray clouds. The deep roots connecting Pushkin's nature with the chaotic whirl vanish. Nekrasov's gray sky lacks horrors, raptures, and abysses; it has nothing but anguished sorrow, although the chaos of Russian reality, which Pushkin had hidden beneath a decorous and playful outwardness, is clearly revealed in Nekrasov.

In Tyutchev's verses, on the other hand, Pushkin's nature becomes so transparent that beneath it one clearly perceives that

> The incorporeal world, terrifying though invisible,
> Seethes now in the nocturnal chaos...
> The ebb flow grows and carries us quickly away
> Into the immensity of the dark waves...
> And we drift, encircled
> By the flaming abyss...[14]

Tyutchev points out to us that the deep roots of Pushkin's poetry have grown spontaneously into the cosmic chaos, this chaos which gazed so frighteningly from the empty eyes of the tragic mask of ancient Greece, deepening the unfolded flight of mythmaking. In its description of Russian nature Tyutchev's art spontaneously echoes the art of ancient Greece: we are struck by how strangely Tyutchev's mythological digressions are combined with his descriptions of Russian nature:

> ....windy Hebe,
> Feeding Zeus' eagle,
> Has, laughing, from the sky poured out
> The loudly foaming goblet onto the earth.[15]

14. Inaccurate quotation from Tyutchev's poem "How sweetly the dark-green garden slumbers" (1835).

15. From Tyutchev's poem "Spring Storm" (1828, 1854).

Splitting apart in Tyutchev, the Pushkin school takes two directions: (1) toward the embodiment of chaos in forms of contemporary reality and (2) toward the embodiment of chaos in the forms of ancient Greece.

A representative of the first direction is Briusov, a representative of the second is Vyacheslav Ivanov, in whose poetry beneath antique school images we hear notes that are familiar to us.

Here we find that the path from the external representation of national wholeness to the search for the ideal incorruptible body of the Russian muse lies through individualism. In the depths of the spirit, "where many-faced horror dwells,"[16] meeting and battle occur. But Nekrasov too, in his own way, points out the chaos of the external conditions of Russian life. The splitting apart of Pushkin's unity is expressed in Tyutchev and Nekrasov in the fact that both of them try but are unable to stay on the surface of Russian reality. They attempt to squeeze their poetry into the narrow frames of political tendencies: Nekrasov into the frame of populism and Tyutchev into the frame of Slavophilism. Moreover, the poet Tyutchev is a government official and an aristocrat, while Nekrasov is a citizen. In Nekrasov's idea of the citizen we find, however, a peculiarly refracted Byronism and Pechorinism,[17] which reveal his connection with Lermontov (to be discussed below). Meanwhile, Tyutchev's aristocratic melody is interrupted by populist notes:

> These poor villages,
> This abject nature form
> My native long-suffering land,
> The land of the Russian people![18]

Tyutchev was also afraid of chaos: "O, do not wake sleeping storms—/Beneath them chaos stirs."[19] We hear his chaos from a distance, as

16. From Briusov's poem "The Fern."

17. Allusion to Pechorin, the Byronic hero of Lemontov's novel *A Hero of Our Time*.

18. From Tyutchev's famous poem "These Poor Villages" (1855).

19. From the poem "What are you wailing about, night wind?" (1835).

if it were an approaching storm at night. His chaos is a chaos of the natural elements that have not been embodied in the minutiae of daily life. On the other hand, the chaotic picture of Russian life drawn by Nekrasov remains superficial. For both Tyutchev and Nekrasov the chaos of the depths is not yet combined with the chaos of the surfaces in such a way that images of visible everyday life form the natural elements and conversely in such a way that everyday images hint at elemental forces. Moreover, Tyutchev's Slavophile aristocratism must merge with Nekrasov's idea of the citizen at a single point of earthy titanism. Before the incorruptible earthy body of Russian poetry can be found, the final revolt of the earthy giants must occur. And it is in fact occurring: in Briusov's poetry elemental forces are producing an earthquake. Into the elemental depths of the rebellious spirit Briusov is introducing interlacements of the external conditions of life. On the other hand, by placing a chaotic content into his sharply delineated and even arid images he is coming closer to a certain inner wholeness. This manifests his blood-kinship with Pushkin: the beginning of the 19th century offers its hand to the beginning of the 20th. Thanks to Briusov we are now able to look at Pushkin's poetry through the prism of Tyutchev's depths. This new point of view opens up a multiplicity of perspectives. The development cycle of the Pushkin school is coming to an end, and the providential character of Russian poetry is being revealed.

The inseparable wholeness of Briusov's form, depicting as it does the earth and the body, is bereft, however, of the fire of the religious heights. The beautiful body of his muse is not yet alive; mechanized by chaos, it is an automaton driven by steam and electricity. Here we are dealing with the steam-driven resurrection of the dead. His muse resembles a demon-possessed woman. She awaits healing in the country of the Gadarenes.[20] She has both an exalted relation to God and a purely bestial relation to the devil: "Come, our God and demi-beast!"[21] If the creatureliness of Briusov's muse is understood in the sense of createdness, at her feet the moon and the stars can appear, as in the case of the Woman clothed in the sun. But if this creatureliness deviates toward "bestiality," at her feet will be the scarlet beast: she

20. See Luke 8:26–39.

21. From Briusov's poem "Temptation" (1902).

will be the Great Whore. The image of the Radiant Woman who is opposed to the beast was born in the depths of the other direction of Russian poetry, the direction which has its origin in Lermontov.

Russian poetry is connected with the poetry of Western Europe. Western European poetry is crowned by cosmic symbols, notably by the symbol of the eternal feminine as represented by Beatrice, Margaret, and others. Another symbol is represented by Prometheus and Manfred. These symbols are given under the veil of estheticism. Russian poetry, borrowing in the person of Lermontov the fundamental traits of the western European spirit, refracts them in its own way with the eastern mysticism that is deeply implanted in the Russian soul. The western European forms express outwardly the mystical experiences of the East. In Lermontov we see the collision of two modes of relation to reality. Individualism battles against universalism. The result will be either the enslavement of mysticism by esthetics (or vice versa) or the fusion of mysticism with esthetics in a theurgic union of religious creativity. In the latter case the result will be the birth from the depths of poetry of a new religion hitherto unknown to the world.

From this comes the tragic element of Lermontov's poetry, giving birth, on the one hand, to the image of the Demon,[22] of Margaret-Tamara,[23] of a gentle dawn smile and eyes full of azure fire; and on the other hand to the image of the infinitely bored Pechorin and to the images of the Unknown Man and the Unknown Woman,[24] who for many years looked at Lermontov "from behind a mysterious cold half-mask."[25] The esthetic shell of the profoundest cosmic symbol, seen by Nietzsche as a tragic mask, is—after the collision of this symbol with the religious creativity of eastern mysticism—transformed by Lermontov into a "half-mask." But the half-mask must be ripped off, for it is a mirage with which the enemy attempts to hide the true nature of the Eternal Woman.

22. Allusion to Lermontov's poem "Demon."

23. Image uniting characters from Goethe's *Faust* and Lermontov's "Demon."

24. The Unknown Man and the Unknown Woman are characters in Lermontov's play *Masquerade*. "The Unknown Woman" (*Neznakomka*) is also the title of Blok's famous 1906 poem.

25. From an 1841 poem by Lermontov.

> Landowner: "I don't know what this is—whether my vision is fogging up from old age or whether something is happening in nature. . . . There's not a single cloud but there seems to be a haze covering everything."
>
> General: "It would be more accurate to say that with his tail the devil is sweeping a fog into God's world."[26]

There is a lot of this gray fog in "A Fairy Tale for Children."[27] Lermontov's demonism, covering with fog the Unknown Woman's countenance, must dissipate and disappear, for the Demon's authentic nature, according to Merezhkovsky's profound insight, consists in petty-bourgeois averageness and grayness. This demonism dissipates in Nekrasov's poetry, being replaced by the idea of the citizen. Here the Pushkin direction of Russian poetry is distorted by a film of Lermontovian demonism. The ripped-off mask scatters into dust and ashes.

On the other hand, the attempt to reconcile Lermontov's tragic individualism with universalism gives birth to Fet's pessimistic pantheism. Fet takes Lermontov's symbols and imbues them with pantheism. If for Lermontov the dawn is a veil hiding the "features of otherness" of the Eternal Unknown Woman, Fet, in contrast, hears the dawn's fading voice:

> Beyond the river your voice fades, burning
> Like the dawn beyond the sea at night.[28]

Liberation from personal will through the esthetic contemplation of the will of the world is the principal mood of Fet's poetry. Here poetry expresses the doctrine of pessimism, but it borrows this doctrine from philosophy. In Russian poetry western European images of creativity strive to merge with mystical experiences and to manifest an image of a renewed religion. That is why the veil of pessimism in Fet is connected with Lermontov's tragic sense, whereas in Heine it is split between *incorporeal* romanticism and purposeless skepticism. That is why Fet is

26. From Solovyov's *Three Conversations*.
27. An 1839 poem by Lermontov.
28. Inaccurate quotation from Fet's poem "To the Singer" (1857).

deeper than Heine. Fet's poetry, however, is not a further development of Lermontov's poetry but only a complement to it; it is a connecting link between Lermontov and European philosophy. Henceforth poetry and philosophy will be inseparable. Henceforth a poet must be more than a singer; he must also be a guide in life. Such was Vladimir Solovyov.

Out of the depths of pessimism Solovyov rose to religious heights. He united poetry with philosophy. For Solovyov the sumptuousness of Fet's pantheism is a veil beneath which Lermontov's tragic sense, cleansed by means of religion, reveals a series of universal historical symbols. The battle of the two principles in man's soul turns out to be the symbol of a universal battle. By illuminating Lermontov's lyricism with this universal consciousness, Solovyov must inevitably rip the half-mask from the face of the Unknown Woman who appeared to Lermontov. And he succeeds in ripping it off. She appears before him in the deserts of sacred Egypt:

> All that was, is, and will be in ages to come,
> All this was embraced here by a single fixed gaze.[29]

This *All* turned out to be *One* image of Feminine beauty—the Bride of the Lamb. The half-mask that was ripped off turned out to be a gray cloud of dust. The enchantment of Lermontov's demonism vanished: it turned out to be nothing but "the devil sweeping a fog into God's world with his tail." According to Merezhkovsky this devil is a sniffler with a head cold and his tail is nothing but the tail of a Great Dane. Through Nekrasov Lermontov's demonism is henceforth embodied in the Pushkinian direction of Russian poetry. This direction culminates in Briusov's poetry, which resurrects the Great Whore, sitting on the scarlet beast. But the scarlet beast is only a phantom—nothing more than dust illuminated by the sun. The beautiful body of Briusov's muse turns out to be a phantom under the rays of the Vision that visited Solovyov. That is why in the poetry of Blok, this follower of Solovyov, reality has a nightmarish quality. Mechanized chaos is transformed into

29. From *Three Meetings*.

emptiness and horror when the Woman clothed in the sun gazes at it. But as for now Her sign is still in heaven. We, however, live on earth. She must come down to us on earth so that earth and heaven can merge in a wedding feast. To Solovyov She appeared as Sophia in the desert of Egypt. She must come to us. Without losing universal unity, She must become our national soul. She must become the unifying principle—*Love*. Her homeland must be not only heaven, but also earth. She must become the organism of love.

But the organization of love that combines person with society must have its focus in mystery. Vyacheslav Ivanov notes very profoundly that the orchestra—a necessary condition of mystery—is a concentration of forms of universal many-voiced suffrage. The organization of these forms is one of the methods of the organization of Love. Suggesting that the community of the future will have a Dionysian basis and pointing out the tragic element in social relations, Ivanov elevates socio-political organization into a religious principle. This tragic element is connected with the cosmic tragedy which consists in the battle of the Woman against the Beast. The incarnate image of the Woman must become the focus of the mystery, wherein the all-unitary principle of humanity is made incarnate. The Woman encountered by Solovyov must come down from heaven and clothe us in the sun of life—in mystery. The chaos made incarnate in Briusov's poetry must become the body of the Woman shining in heaven.

Nekrasov's idea of the citizen was destined to be rooted in Dionysian soil. Tyutcvhev's chaos was destined to engender a bright daughter from its darkness. Let us hope that Briusov's muse will leave the country of the Gadarenes, that is, those places where mechanized Americanism sings its terrible songs with factory whistles, electrical bells, and ceaselessly bursting grenades suspended from iron rods on streets where trams like iron lizards run rapidly along the rails. This is the metropolis of the Gadarenes. This is where she strolls amid the smoke and horse trams.

> From the tram she strode down like a goddess.

Does this mean that an iron lizard, a beast, serves as her pedestal? But who is she?

Yes! I saw you in the crimson light
Wearing a golden tiara. Like a proud empress
You were celebrating your victory in the conquered capital.[30]

Briusov's muse strides from the tram to the crimson, whereas Blok's muse, having appeared to us in the crimson, strides toward—the tram.

The two muses begin a frightening duet: their eyes meet. The azure rays of one pierce "the nocturnal darkness of empty eyes." From the lips of the other there wafts "something beastly, the quiet of caves and the desolation of cliffs." Between them crawls the tram—the iron lizard. All around stand the champions of the Beast and of the Woman. It is not by chance that Blok says:

Frightening and full of mystery will be
The unearthly masks covering the faces.[31]

The final veil covering Russian poetry must now be ripped off. The true faces will be revealed for all time. She will appear—the One

...before whom the great magician of my land
Languishes and gnashes his teeth.[32]

Everywhere in Blok's poetry we encounter the attempt to embody a supratemporal vision in forms of space and time. She is already among us, with us, embodied, living, near, this muse of Russian Poetry who has been recognized at last, this muse who has turned out to be the Sun in which the rays of the newly revealed religion have intersected, this religion the battle for which will be the task of our entire life. Here she is, sitting with a dear and radiant smile, as if there is nothing mysterious in her, as if the great insights of poets and mystics have nothing to do with her. But at the moment of secret peril, when our soul is attacked by the storms of raging chaos and is so afraid "amid the unknown steppes,"[33] her smile chases away the storm clouds; the bliz-

30. From Briusov's poem "The Empress" (1901).

31. From Blok's poem "You are holy but I do not believe You" (1902).

32. Inaccurate quotation from prayer four of Blok's cycle "Prayers" (1904). The "great magician" is Briusov.

zard's chaotic columns spread obediently as white snow as soon as she directs at them her azure gaze, burning with the dawn of immortality. And then she departs again, quiet and severe, into "distant rooms."[34] And the heart implores that she return.

She appeared to Solovyov in the deserts of Egypt. In Blok's verse she already appears among us, not recognized by the world, recognized by few. Henceforth the heavenly vision unites heaven and earth and is reflected in the minutiae of life. But not all life is yet subject to her. Chaos that has not become her body still rages all around. The chaos contains malicious forces that oppose her power. Focusing on chaotic reality, Blok's poetry becomes nightmarish: a black little man runs all over the city and runs up to a house where men at round tables are shouting without rhyme or reason; toward morning a cross is formed in the rosy clouds and a grotesque dwarf in a red dress-coat floats by, carried by springtime torrents streaming in the street. This is the dragon, the many-faced serpent gathering his forces against Her. Afraid that She will defeat the world, he pursues Her into Her Habitations.

The Lermontovian and Pushkinian currents of Russian poetry, having reached full definition in Briusov and Blok, must merge into an amazing unity. But how? Through free unification or through subordination? In the latter case we would have a battle between two realities. On the one hand, the integral wholeness of Briusov's realism with its pronounced note of Astartism is transformed in Blok's poetry into a nightmare when his muse looks at a world not subordinate to her. On the other hand, Her realest all-unity is, from Briusov's point of view, an incorporeal vision. Along the boundaries where these two opposite points of view meet we see oscillations and duality; battle ensues, fears grow, the chimeras of ancient Greece are resurrected, and the Gorgon of war laughs insanely with a red laughter. Naudeau writes that "in our contemporary war everything is mysterious, scattered, remote, invisible, abstract. . . . One is constantly deceived by a phantasmagoria." Phantasmagoria, mirage—that is what invariably grows out of the collision of the two opposite principles of the world. The red hor-

33. From Pushkin's poem "Demons."

34. From an early sophianic poem by Blok.

ror of battle laughing on the fields of Manchuria and the rooster of fire crowing in accompaniment to the battle—all this is only the outer veil of the universal battle in which the splintered depths of our souls are sinking. All this constitutes "the mask of the red death"[35] into which the "grimace of the world" observed by Nietzsche is being transformed.

We said that three masks have to be ripped off the Countenance of the Russian muse. The first to fly off is the Godlike mask of Pushkin's muse, behind which chaos hides. The second is the half-mask covering the Countenance of the Heavenly Vision. The third is the Cosmic Mask, the "mask of the red death" conditioning the cosmic battle between the Beast and the Woman. This battle constitutes the content of the tragic. Western European poetry expresses the outward character of this battle; the tragic is the formal definition of the apocalyptic battle. Building a bridge to religion, Russian poetry is the unifying link between the tragic world-view of European man and the final church of believers gathered together to battle the Beast.

In both of its currents Russian poetry implants itself deep into universal life. The problem raised by this poetry can be solved only by the transformation of Earth and Heaven into the city of New Jerusalem. The apocalypse of Russian poetry is brought about by the approach of the End of Universal History. Only here can we find a solution to the Pushkinian and Lermontovian mysteries.

IV

We believe that You will be revealed to us, that the fogs of October will dissipate and the yellow thaws of February will cease. Let people think that You are still asleep in the icy grave:

> You repose in the white grave.
> With a smile You call: do not wake
> The golden curls on my brow,
> The golden icon on my breast.[36]

35. Allusion to Poe's story "The Masque of the Red Death."
36. From Blok's poem "Here they are, the steps leading to the grave" (1904).

Not so! You have risen.

You promised to appear all in *rose*, and our souls bow before You in prayer and hear Your prayerful sighing in the dawns, those scarlet icon-lamps.

Come!

It's time: the world has ripened like a sweet plump golden fruit. Without You the world is in anguish.

Come!

The Crisis of Culture[1]

I

Above the green streaming of the Rhine, you can clearly see the hills; the Rhine rushes past houses, bushes and hills; past tile roofs piercing the mists with a dirty orange hue as the setting sun strikes them; and the Münster Cathedral, brightly flaming and brightly stony, rises before you; the grape leaves glow red (it's already fall)—they spread themselves like a rosy stream on the slightly flaming gray tower which rises stonily into the purple air in this evening hour; the miniature dragon in the ornamental pond opens wide its maw—at the idle bunch of eroded violet noses.

This is Basel.

It is a venerable university town. The university library draws you in with the comfort of its deserted rooms, with the cornucopia of its old volumes. Leaning over them, I'd submerge myself in the intricate arabesques of Raymond Lully's thought, striving, through *Ars brevis* and Bruno's commentaries, to penetrate the *Ars Magna* of this capricious Catalan sage, troubadour, and martyr.

Basel is a university town, but no sharp word will ever cut through its thick, heavy air, saturated with moisture and disgorging torrents of rain from October to May (the climate is awful!).

Words can only crawl here; they trudge heavily through the puddles, get stuck, and fall on their faces. A group of hideous inhabitants, after staring at the sunset, creeps into a lousy, smoke-filled tavern, followed by a gimpy-legged cretin.[2]

1. First published Petrograd, 1920. Some material in this essay has been omitted.

2. Bely literally takes this to mean a dwarfed and deformed person suffering from a condition caused by a congenital deficiency of thyroid hormones common in Alpine lands. He observed a number of such individuals in Basel.

2

Old Basel is full of a momentous past and a momentous future, which straddles it from its outskirts with the turquoise domes of the Johannes Building, which I too (ineptly and timidly) helped to build.[3]

Living near Basel for two and a half years, I came to understand that this was precisely the place where Nietzsche had to compose fragments of *The Birth of Tragedy* and to feel for the first time the crisis of culture: "At the age of thirty-six, I was at the lowest ebb of my life. . . . I was still alive, but could not see three paces beyond me. At that time . . . I had left my Basel professorship. . . . To observe from the point of view of a sick man *healthier* notions and values and, conversely, to observe the work of the instinct of degeneration from the point of view of the fullness and self-confidence of a richer life—such was my prolonged exercise, my true experience.[4]

Nietzsche's presence is imprinted in the air by a crash inaudible to the ears: September spite and September sunlight fill me in Basel with thoughts of Nietzsche. When at sunset I stand above the green streaming of the Rhine, then in the saturated and threatening air that whispers to me, I clearly hear that the birth of the tragedy can be found in *Nietzsche's sickness.*

Divergence with contemporaneity, the crisis of culture, is what he experiences here, as well as a profound disenchantment with Germans. Here, we see Jacob Burckhardt, an old man, tearing himself away from his books and in agitation dragging himself up to the lectern to warn the young people against the pompous fanfares of arrogant imperialism. And we see Nietzsche applauding him and announcing a series of lectures on culture; we see Nietzsche's agonizing break with Wagner, his abasement, the smashing of his hopes; we see his sister taking him from here and his life fading here at the age of 75. From here he writes: "I have suffered for thirty consecutive hours"; and from here the sick man is transported closer to the air of the mountains.

3. The Johannes Building was the original name of the Goetheanum, designed by Rudolf Steiner and built by members of Steiner's Anthroposophical Society. Bely was a member then and took part in the building.

4. From *Ecce Homo.*

3

Here repose the ashes of the greatest of our contemporary poets, a poet who died too soon: Christian Morgenstern hovers like a star above the beginnings of the new culture. I had the great good fortune once to shake his hand; he was already near death. When I shook his hand, he answered me with a gaze I will never forget. We met in Leipzig, at a course of lectures seeking to discover the meaning of the Holy Grail. Leipzig was where both Wagner and Goethe (when he was ill) were initiated into life. Morgenstern was like an older brother to me, united with me by our mutual love for our teacher.[5] His entire being was transfigured by touching the spiritual science[6]—the distant star that still glimmers before me: Christian *Morgen-Stern*.[7]

Clearly imprinted in my memory are the shining gazes of his enormous azure eyes, his unearthly smile, his slender transparent hand, extended like a helping hand into the future.

In those unforgettable years I visited, near Leipzig, the remains of one who for many years was a radiant source of comfort for me, as he was for Morgenstern: the remains of Friedrich Nietzsche (I still retain the leaves of eternal ivy that I plucked at his grave). The grave of this dear deceased, the fact that it is the homeland of the radiant Goethe, the enormous mystery of the Grail, the meeting with Morgenstern—these are the things that make Leipzig memorable for me.

But the center of my life was Basel, where, like Nietzsche, I was tormented by knowledge of the depths of degeneration in myself. In Basel, the morning light of Morgenstern shepherded me like a guiding star through the courses of spiritual science to the Johannes Building, to its two domes, gleaming turquoise now. Like thunder the teacher's words resounded there, as well as the words of our contemporary Eckhart, Karl Bauer, whose profound judgments I venerate.

It is possible that in this Basel I buried myself forever, but it is also possible that I was spiritually born there. The remembrances of my childhood, "my life," are a tale of my distant future: in Bergen I saw

5. Rudolf Steiner.
6. Steiner's Anthroposophy.
7. "Morning star" in German.

enormous bursts of light, and Morgenstern glimmered past me as a memory of Bergen. Meanwhile here in Dornach (near Basel) a crown of thorns was placed on my head; and, sick with suffering like Nietzsche, I rushed into the mountains.

The crises of contemporary culture that led to war, the thunder of war, and the war itself I experienced with my double near Basel.

4

Friedrich Nietzsche lived in Basel. He is the knife-edge of all culture; its tragic crisis is contained in the crisis of his life. "Some day my name will be linked with the memory of something enormous—with the memory of a crisis never before seen on earth, of the profoundest collision of conscience."[8] That is what culture uttered with his lips; with this explosion he blew himself up, he blew up the "German" in himself (because "they are intolerable for him"[9]); he blew up the "good and kind" man in himself, "for the good and kind cannot create anything, but are the beginning of the end."[10] He blew up the human being in himself at the very moment when culture had achieved an extraordinary range: "On that perfect day when all things achieve ripeness and the grape clusters are not the only things that turn red, I looked back, I looked forward, and I had never before seen so many good things at once."[11]

My first visit to Basel (I remember it as if it were yesterday) was in September: in those perfect days I was awestruck by the magnificent music of the Gospel of Mark resounding in Steiner's lectures.[12] "The voice of one crying in the wilderness, Prepare ye the way of the Lord, make his paths straight."[13] *That voice was Nietzsche.*

I remember that those days in Basel the grape leaves were turning red, and the sun cast a ray on my life; later on, to myself I narrated "my life," my first childish experiments at consciousness—I did this at the

8. From *Ecce Homo.*

9. Ibid.

10. Ibid.

11. Ibid.

12. In Basel in September 1912, Bely attended Steiner's lectures on the Gospel of Mark.

13. Mark 1:3.

hour when the voice of the Gospel of Mark thundered deafeningly over the 20th century: "there shall not be left one stone upon another, that shall not be thrown down" (13:2).

"Tell us, when shall these things be?" (13:4)

"When ye shall hear of wars and rumours of wars, be ye not troubled: for such things must needs be; but the end shall not be yet. For nation shall rise against nation, and kingdom against kingdom . . . and there shall be famines and troubles. . . . Now the brother shall betray the brother to death, and the father the son; and children shall rise up against their parents, and shall cause them to be put to death. . . . But when ye shall see the abomination of desolation . . . let them that be in Judaea flee to the mountains: And let him that is on the housetop not go down into the house. . . . For in those days shall be affliction, such as was not from the beginning of the creation. . . . And except that the Lord had shortened those days, no flesh should be saved . . . when ye shall see these things come to pass, know that it is nigh. . . ." (13:7, 8, 12, 14, 15, 19, 20, 29).

Near Basel, I narrated "my life" to myself when the thorns pierced my brow—in agonizing Dornach; the guns thundered there, from Alsace, informing the whole world of the fall and destruction of the buildings of culture.

I heard the voice of the one who had suffered here like me: "Politics . . . will dissolve into spiritual warfare. . . . The forms . . . of the old society will be blown up. . . . There will be wars such as the world has never seen. . . . I am dynamite. . . . I know my lot."[14]

The Rhine flows furiously in Basel: here, overturned into streams, the radiant sun weaves golden rings, flying, spilling and breaking into streams against the stony shores populated by a multitude of Nibelungen waging fierce wars with the gods for the Rhine gold; the whole history of capitalism, which has brought us to the horrors of the world catastrophe and the destruction of contemporary culture, can be viewed as a materialization of the solar flecks playing on the surface of these waters: the return of the gold to the Rhine can be viewed as a return of the riches belonging to the natural elements—back to the natural elements.

14. From *Ecce Homo*.

And Nietzsche, having seen the value of the gold out of which emperors and generals were cast in Germany, rejected this gold; he conjured the return of this materialized treasure, this gold, back to the waters; he foresaw the gold of the sun precisely where for us the sun itself is a heavy and inert metal.

He aspired to be Siegfried: there is a legend that Wagner gave his hero the traits of the ex-professor Nietzsche who, at the boundary between two epochs, raised over Europe a terrible sword—the sword of spiritual war.

"I walk among people as if I were walking among ruins of the future—of the future that I see."[15]

"I am an unprecedented messenger of good news: I know tasks which are so high that till now there have been no concepts for them. With me, there is again hope for the first time."[16]

5

Eternal books are like springs of water. A gap of years stretches between two life-giving swallows from a book which is such a spring. You open to a page and water spills out from between the lines; pouring onto the desk, it flows down like a waterfall. The whole room is flooded with streams of water; breaking through the windows, its foaming waves carry you outside. Flowing with them, you rush over the stones, multiplying the sparkling radiance and being flung like a heap of diamonds toward the shore. The vivaciously flowing word, producing a rainbow above the splashes, grows in the air into an archangel who throws bridges from earth to heaven.

6

Three books "accompany me": the Gospels, *Zarathustra*, and Steiner's *Way of Initiation*. Everydayness spreads its sands and they shut off the springs. I change habitations: Sicily flashes before me, but *Zarathustra* is with me.... Or having climbed up onto a flat roof in a forgotten

15. From *Thus Spoke Zarathustra*.
16. From *Ecce Homo*.

village near Tunis, I observe on the square below me a bunch of Arabs with their turquoise bournouses gleaming into the turquoise African night; the soft sobbing of a tam-tam reminds me of the desert, and *Zarathustra* is with me. Or, amidst the glaciers of auroral Norway, where purple moss covers the green noble stones and where from a half-frozen pond I pick up a reindeer antler, *Zarathustra* is with me there too. He is also with me in distractingly noisy Paris and in awful Berlin. Flashing before me are Jerusalem and Cairo, Petersburg and Moscow, Cologne, memorable (for me) Bruges, affable Brussels, mysterious Nuremberg, Christiania, Copenhagen, turreted Prague, pensive Strasbourg, laughing Munich. Countries change, but my unceasing anguish is always with me. *Zarathustra* is with me (I used to travel with Kant, but he was too heavy to carry around, so I dropped him).

I like to travel with an unchanging center—i.e., my precious trinity of books. Every city deposits its gift in me—Norway its chrysolite and Munich its turquoise. Translucent chrysolite, turquoise, and beryl (Copenhagen) I offer as a gift to my precious trinity. Refracting, it reflects me—in myself. It is like a homeland to me, a promise that my wanderings will end. Raised above myself, I find myself in it; and in myself I verify myself, in the spring of waters emerging from between the pages. All the things that flashed past me and all the things that have fallen into my depths re-emerge with these waters: the Norwegian chrysolites flow out in green waves and the sky-blue turquoises spill out their dreams. The sun really appeared—a golden stream; a city in my soul—a leadening stream.

7

All great books are transparent and alive. They come to life as creations woven of iridescent sparks. Do you know the state of consciousness of thought that strains itself until a spark leaps out of your eyes? This spark will suddenly flash between you and some random object at which you had been looking absentmindedly; and after flashing, it will fade. Listen: Was your thought so intense that it squeezed "a spark from your eyes"? If not, you'll probably laugh at me; but in that case you're not a philosopher: Philosophy is a living country full of inexpressible landscapes where the visible world is deposited as a grain in your thought. The country of philosophy is like the earthy, ardent heart of some electrical creature stretching from universe to universe: The creature has unfurled its enormous wings; thousands of luminous eyes are looking inward and screaming with bright light:

"I!"

"I!"

"I!"

"I!"

"I!"

This multiplicity of "I's" is a flowing multiplicity in an archangel's thought: all thoughts are archangelic...

8

If you keep reflecting on one and the same basic theme, your reflections over the months will merge and it will flash through your mind that it is as though you keep returning, for example, in the mornings to the same work and continuing it. And between two reflections a measured day passes: let it take its course; the feeling of thought will not enter into it and change the order of the usual day; you will be more businesslike and sober: at the moment of the reflections your cares will recede.

The reflections of the mornings merge for you, turning into bursts from the wellsprings of thoughts; and there will come the most enormous moment of all, when the source of waters in the depths of the reflection will splash outward and expanding the wellspring of thought (till the spark flies from your eyes) you will see how deep is the flowing source of thought. It will splash instantaneously and pour into your usual thoughts; and your thoughts will start moving and take you with them. Flow with your thoughts and you will no longer say: "I think." Instead, you will say: "Thinking me up, my thoughts think me." I am thought now as a hierarchical entity: the observation and description of the occurring processes, the exact copy of them, sketches for me countries of *Theories* casting shadows where I outline the shadows with charcoal on the white pasteboard of my receptivity. When you call yourself a theoretician, I throw you the question: Have you ever been in the country of thought?

We do not know life-giving thoughts: our usual thoughts are not thoughts; they are instruments by which we drill through thick strata down to a meeting with an underground source emitting jets of artesian water from a crevice of concepts.

Our usual logic is a pitiful parcel of land on which we, the proprietors, ordinarily plant only "vegetables" of prejudices.

But the eternal books are neither soil nor vegetables. They are rushing streams that undermine the foundations and rip the letters and lines of pages, gushing up like fountains and carrying us through the windows—into the immensities of the cosmos.

We do not know the sources that intersect all the domains of measured thought: beneath the soil of thought, the impression awaiting us from the sources of thought is incomparable:

Suddenly, thought expands. Those undergoing this expansion experience a catastrophe threatening to cast them into illness. It seems to them that their thoughts are no longer their own. Thinking themselves, their thoughts begin to tremble, seethe, and run in the labyrinths of the brain, like the manyfold multiplicity of ants in an anthill. Out of numberless passages they crawl; they crawl after prey, and then they return.

The thoughts think themselves: they have flown out of the usual circle of consciousness, which is ripped apart by the rushing stream of bubbling images. The stale "I" is submerged and dissolved in thought; the "I" is grabbed, ripped out, and carried off; when it attempts to return and rise to the surface, it lands in an alien consciousness.

The experiments at exercises with thought displace the boundaries of consciousness and, diving into the sources of thought, teach us to rise again to the surface, into our neighbor, to co-experience his "I" and say to him:

"I am thou."

They teach us to dive again and return into our brain through the obscure remembrance of a state of consciousness adjacent to you (outwardly outlined by your skull); and this clarity of thought grows.

9

When geniuses talk about culture, what they say is sharpened to the extreme, like a razor's edge. Their aphorisms compress entire libraries—of unwritten books that raise the curtain that veils the future.

The Birth of Tragedy, for example, is an aphorism in which *the spirit of the time* speaks. This speech of the high mountains is unceasing; Nietzsche heard a chance phrase of it and formed his new view of Greece, but there was much he did not understand! If we were able to ascend to the circles of the 20th century, it would appear to us that the truths of this century belong to the 15th century. Truly, there is nothing more majestic that our contemporary events; alas, they are usually taken to mean the distant past digested by the gastric juices of insignificant little souls; the "products" of the culture in which we live are nothing but refuse.

I am confronted by a swarm of truths which are only little mountains and which form the mountain ridge of contemporaneity. But, alas, our contemporaries call these little mountains the "horizons of the future"; in the worst case they call these antiquities of truth a chimera. What would they say if they could really see contemporaneity? I was once ridiculed, but now my books are often quoted as an authoritative source, which tempts me to make the instinctive gesture of *rejecting myself*. In truth, my books are only a tale about "objects" accessible to the attention of everyone; but no one pays attention to the facts I have observed.

I used to say: "Look, there's a cloud." But people would laugh, and years would pass and thunderstorms would roll by; and instead of believing in the "objects" of my observation, my admirers display my weighty tomes: Here we have *Symbolism* and over there we have *Petersburg*.[17] The horizon of my visions is deliberately shut off from their gazes by my pages. At the horizon of knowledge there is a new turbulent life; the sun rises and sets; dawns gleam and clouds rise; that to which I speak, "contemporaneity," is a chimera for everyone.

10

In twenty years or so it will be revealed that Augustine is a Protestant without a trace of Catholicism. Through him, Plotinus flows into the Middle Ages; he contains Goethe's Faust as well as Wagner-Kant; in

17. Two of Bely's most important works. *Symbolism* is a book of critical and philosophical essays and *Petersburg* is a famous novel.

him, one hears the sigh of Bach's fugues. The subtlest combination of the "contemporaneities" of the modern epoch is already contemporary: at the beginning of the epoch our days were already contained in the 6th century.[18] Augustine was equal to it; all others lagged behind the times.

In Augustine the battle against the Manichaean teacher, Faustus, did not end in victory. It continued[19] and triumphed over Augustine's consciousness; he suffered defeat in his subconscious.

II

That which nowadays is taken as truth has been refuted by the spirit of the events of culture.

There is a tendency to link the Renaissance with mysticism: the humanists were supposedly preceded by mystics who represented a diminution of scholasticism—*the dark past of thought*; but in the explorations of our own time this *dark past* constitutes light: we venerate the bright flashes of Abelard's thought.

Bernard of Clairvaux and Hugh of Saint Victor are, in our opinion, more mystical than Eckhart and Boehme, who are not so much mystics as "occultists," "scholars," and "thinkers." True, the theological "formulations" were, for the most part, in harmony with the mystics' explorations of the "depths." Thus, having ripped the heavens into two parts (knowable and unknowable), theology attempts to formulate the knowable heaven, whereas mysticism plumbs the unknowableness of the unknowable part.

Denying the sundering of the heavens into two parts, scholasticism proclaimed that it had the right to explore it freely. Theology and mysticism formed a cunning union against scholasticism, and the latter fragmented, producing "Thomism." Before "Thomism" scholasticism contained the sources of the Renaissance and clearly foreshadowed the 17th century—in the agonies of Abelard's metaphysical conscience, where Augustine seethed with his freedom of spirit.

18. Bely probably meant the 4th or 5th century. Augustine's years are 354–430.
19. See Augustine's *Contra Faustum*. (Bely's note)

Augustine, however, is not a saint but only "blessed" (an indicator of the very typical restraint exhibited by all Catholics, Jesuits, and theological rats, for whom he is, of course, very suspect). If he had been born later, he would have shared Lully's fate. "Ars Lulliana" covered Europe and Raymond's work was considered saintly; but later Lully's books were burned by the Catholic church; and it is not by chance that Bruno, Lully's great champion, was burned at the stake—and when he burned, all of scholasticism burned too, together with its progenitor, Augustine.

And so, for the church he is a Protestant.

Protestantism is deeper than its main flow, Luther. It had many sources, its springs breaking through the stony, joyless soils of the 6th, 9th, and 10th centuries; it grew strong in the 12th century, was the source of Italian culture, and was etched into humanity by Dürer's woodcuts. Its name is "Christism."

The "woman clothed in the sun" represents the early Christian community: over a number of centuries this woman is squeezed around us by the official church and becomes the "Nuremberg" lady, the "iron" lady, an instrument of torture: a case with knives protruding inside. But outside the case, outside the church, outside the enclosure built around her, the woman clothed in the sun shines out to us: the Madonna of Italy, the "womanness" of the woman. Outside the constricting enclosure of the church we see the shining in paints of the religious foundations of man, where "He" is unfathomably painted into the hearts of people and expresses, outside the church, the transfiguration of the human subconscious unto its fusion with beings of the cosmic spheres. We see this in Dante's Beatrice and in Leonardo's "Madonna" and "Christ." "Christs" and "Madonnas" stroll among us like people on the canvases and frescos of Italy, spilling their painterly impulse not into the visible church but into the hidden, mysterious church whose unrevealed name is "culture." Official Christianity enters into battle with this mysteriously in-painted Christophoric freedom—with the "Christism" of culture in which this mystery of Christ is expressed openly in a multiplicity of distortions (the Russian khlysts are an example). The battle is between "Christianity" and "Christism," later manifested in the battle between the Renaissance and the Inquisition. Herein is foreshadowed the highly improbable possibility of transfiguring life into a "mystery"; and through the battle of social relations there enters into the consciousness the "mystery-drama," whose end comes later: only in the Solar Temple of future culture will we see a transfiguration of life in which the four estates will speak with the prophetic voices of the four hierophants of culture. In Steiner's mystery-drama we see: the Solar Temple; the hierophants Benedictus, Theodosius, Romanus, and Retardus stand facing one another; they preside as representatives of humanity.[20]

The Solar Temple comes later. This solar temple or "city" shined forth clearly in the Alexandrian period of thought; and later it shined in Italy in the "*Civitas Solis*," but the "*Civitas Solis*" was realized as the *imperium* in Rome. In Italy this City shined forth solarly in Michelangelo's architectural designs (in the Italian architecture at which the Renaissance failed); its degradation is in Machiavelli and its symbolism is in Campanella's "socialism."

12

Till now "Christism" remains a stimulus of culture. Note some intimate elements in this culture: the powers of the Madonna act mysteriously in the simple "Fornarina,"[21] and the great powers of Christ are inscribed mysteriously in Faust. This shift of human powers (or sin) may be a power of tenderness or love that has not found its channel.

We find this to be characteristic: Christ silently traced something on the ground before the woman who had sinned. That which he mysteriously traced became a clear hint in the culture of Italy; it secretly spilled over into "Protestantism" and, unbeknownst to anyone, it guided the history of the revolt of culture in its battle with the church.

The future (perhaps the 25th century) flared up in the 15th century: the *ray of rays* was the Renaissance and the star anticipating the "ray of rays" and invisibly illumined by it—that star ascended from the 1st to the 4th centuries in... Alexandria.

20. See Steiner's mystery-drama "At the Gates of Initiation." (Bely's note)
21. A painting by Raphael also known as "The Portrait of a Young Woman."

13

The thought of the ancient Greeks can be likened to an image: its materialization would mean the resurrection of Apollo and Venus. But the materialization of the thought of the Alexandrian Greeks would mean the resurrection of images of magnificent Italy: Alexandria constituted a giant leap from the thought of antiquity. It is before us: the woods encircling the Solar Temple (or City); the unfinished Temple concealed by them (the "idea" of Plotinus)—the Madonna; the "one" of the 5th century BC—Apollo; the "one" of the 3rd century AD—the Christ of Leonardo's "Last Supper"; between the two, in the intermediate centuries, the horrible convulsions of suffering and strengthening thought, reaching their peak in the spasms of Alexandria, or Michelangelo's "Last Judgment," where the enraged Apollo (or Christ) condemns the doomed body: the wave of burnt bodies is decadence; at the same time, there is the inner light consuming the body, unto the spirit, and penetrating into the spirit.

The convulsions of Alexandrian culture foreshadowed the excesses of the cult of personhood in the Italian Renaissance; and the imminent "Christism" of culture shines forth with a mysterious light in the feasts of this life, "feasts" which will become a "last supper" where the invited Guest is man in man. He is still the Unrecognized one and wanders within us; and we, wandering pilgrims, seek a meeting with the Guest.

The culture of the recent centuries (from the 16th to the 20th) is a pilgrimage; and it finds expression in the "pilgrim."

In the Borgias and Medici, in the strangely original popes (Nicholas, Leo, Julius), in the refinement, in the "syncretism" of the Renaissance feasts, there are as yet no *pilgrimages*; in the feasts the tragedy of transubstantiated personhood is ripening, and soon Man (Faust, pale Hamlet, and Manfred) will be revealed in it and the joys of the feast will dissipate: the hall of the feast will become the sorcerer's cellar which we encounter in *Faust*.

Faust is saved.

14

The whole tragedy of the Renaissance is exposed by Faust. But in Goethe's *Faust* (in the last scene) Faust falls apart into a corruptible garment destined to be consumed by fire ("Und wär er von Asbest, Er ist nicht reinlich")[22] and into one who is resurrected into spiritual life; and from the heights of the spiritual world we see that Faust—having covered the 16th and 17th centuries with the inventions of Galileo, Copernicus, and Kepler—colorfully flowed into the worlds of the spirit as an enormous musical wave whose source was Bach; and the vivification of the northern part of Central Europe by the Italian stream is a vivification of Faust who is "faithful to the Lord"[23] by the spirit of scientific creativity. The mystery of this creativity lies in the "thump"[24] of the musical stream.

This "thump" is manifested later as—the music of Bach. I know that what I am saying is paradoxical to the extreme; but only with such paradoxes is it possible to touch the enormous unrevealed mystery of European culture; what I have glimpsed is a mass of unrevealed relations between the scientific, esthetic, philosophical, and religious life of Europe in recent centuries. I know that herein is contained a library of unwritten books; but when they are written, everyone will agree with me. "He who has ears to hear, let him hear."

15

Bach manifested the impulses that have vivified European culture from the time of Augustine to our own time: the revolution has taken place; it has been accomplished within Christianity. The streams of the life-giving impulse, Bach, broke through the soil like artesian springs and spilled out the science and art of the Renaissance.

"Christism," as an impulse, circulated through the network of the blood vessels of the massive organism of Europe—outside the church and the dogmas. It splashed out in artesian streams, emerging in the legend of the Grail (in the 12th century); a network of dry channels remained but the life-giving streams broke through the soil, revealing

22. "Even if they were made of asbestos, they still would not be neat and tidy." That is what the perfect angels say of their earthly remains.

23. From Faust: "Prologue in Heaven."

24. In Russian: "bakh." ("Bakh" is the Russian transliteration of Bach)

the channels to be a form of the departed impulse (the impulse now came back to life in another place of the soul's landscape). Gothic architecture—the frames of the cathedrals—became the form of the mysterious impulse.

The interdependence of ogives running toward the center is like the interdependence of vessels (the arteries and veins of the soul's blood system). In Gothic architecture, in the cathedrals of Strasbourg, Aachen, Cologne, and Reims, the struggles of Augustine's soul were shaped in stone: thus, the mystery of the 6th century,[25] his contemporaneity, became manifest in the 15th century; the cathedrals are the frames of Augustine's soul, of his self-conscious soul.

Greek philosophy is the life of the reasoning soul. Its architectural form is the colonnade and portico; on its harmonious columns stands a triangle. That is the form of the Greek temple; its apex symbolizes the "one" of Parmenides, Plato, and Aristotle; and its columns symbolize concepts (Aristotle's categories).

The philosophy of our time is the philosophy of the self-conscious soul: this soul of contemporaneity was first awakened in Augustine; in the 15th century the play of its life created a perfect architectural form: the Gothic cathedral; and having created it, this soul flowed out of this form (out of the church) into formlessness, into the revolt of Europe's seething culture.

What came out of the form? What flowed out of the cathedral, out of the church, into culture?

The melodious musical fugue.

Thus: the cathedrals of Aachen, Cologne, and Reims are frozen fugues; Schlegel's definition of music ("flowing architecture") is mathematically exact.

Where once the mysterious impulse of scholasticism sprang forth, one saw in the 15th century a hierarchy, a fugue, of soaring arches; at the boundary of the 17th and 18th centuries there occurred a further shaping of the impulse or the removal of new seals from it. Those seals were the music of thought (modern philosophy), and the thought of the music was Bach.

One can say straight out: the philosophy of the modern period is a

25. See note 18 on p. 115.

musical spreading forth and gradation of the monumental cathedrals; it is a growth from the 6th century, the visibleness of the hidden life-impulse: *Cor Ardens*.

At one time everything beat in the flaming heart of the "one." This "one" was Paul (the apostle); his disciple was Augustine; from the flame of Augustine's heart the tree of our culture stretched its rays: scholasticism, the Gothic, music, thought.

Augustine is the unrecognized flame of the entire secular culture; and Faust is born in this flame.

Unconsciously assimilating Faust into himself, Goethe with his consciousness struggles furiously against the Manichean teacher—Faustus.

And so his work proceeds through the centuries from the teacher Faustus—through Plotinus, the apostle Paul, scholasticism, the Gothic, Bach; through all of philosophy to Goethe's *Faust*.

Das Unbeschreibliche
Hier ist's getan.[26]

16

It is paradoxical that from Plotinus flowed the majestic form of the later cathedrals: here the ogives and arches are streams from a musical source. Somewhere over there, on the pinnacles of Plotinus' spirit, the "one" of his thought pierced the Platonic heaven of ideas like a needle: plunging through the aperture of thought, the ecstasy of intuition flowed directly into the blood of man; and Paul's "Vision" was revealed in the distances beyond the ecstasy. And Paul's Athenian school expressed the gradations of the down-flying streams of Divinity in the description of the angelic hierarchies.[27] All this, falling on us, comes to life and seethes in Augustine's intensely flaming heart; it materializes through reason (of the Scholastics) in masses of stone: in cathedrals, in the Gothic.

If we were to clothe Plotinus's philosopheme in a flesh of stones, the

26. "The undescribable, here it is done." (From *Faust*)
27. Allusion to *On the Celestial Hierarchy* of Dionysius the Areopagite.

cathedral of Strasbourg would rise before us. That which was still fluid (in reason and in stone) flowed out of the Gothic form as chorale and fugue, and continued to burrow like a stream though man's blood.

Out of Bach flowed music; in Bach all of Beethoven was sung.

Out of the life-giving source in the 1st century flowed the musical stream: state and church were its deposits; as for itself, it was deposited as "culture."

Culture is the green growth over the stream of the religious new impulse. And this impulse is Christ.

17

We clearly see the materialization of the impulse in Alexandrian culture; its materialization was Rome; here the *one* of the entire synthetic philosophy materialized into the *unity* of the gigantic state, in which the attempt was made to fuse synthetically the multiplicity of national cultures; the image of the gigantic Empire was formed only starting with the 1st century.

The world Empire, Rome, was the materialization: it was the distorted frame of Alexandrian synthetism.

It is paradoxical that the state is truly a premature materialization of music; here the mystery of human relations, the free development of the latter, the counterpoint of variations is rationally registered *as law* and *as duty*; and therefore we can say that *law, duty,* and *right*, together with the categorical imperative, are, of course, products of a philosophy of the state. Kant's philosophy clearly represents an imperialism of the country of thought; the rationalism of the philosophy of the new period is rooted in the ethical principle of thought: it is the "Rome" of the country of thought, and this Rome has shackled the minds of German philosophers.

That which the schools of Plotinus and Philo had worked on found a distorted application to life in the work of the gigantic Augustus, who created a social frame for the uncomprehended mystery of the soul. Between the descent of the Logos into the souls of men and the endeavors of Augustus Caesar in this period—there is a mysterious link.

But obvious here is a shift of perspective.

18

That which was mysterious in Alexandrian culture poured down and lived beneath the soil of "Rome"; it was catacombic. One can truly say that the *imperium* was blown up by the catacomb and emerged as the Church; the place where the emperor had once built a temple to Mithras (in the Alexandrian period of culture) was now crowned by the Temple of St. Peter; that which had emerged from underground materialized a second time. The theocratic principle, like the *imperium*, mixed up the perspectives: like "Rome" the ecclesiastical State was ripped apart; but from the rips, as from vivid Gothic windows, there again splashed the Alexandrian impulses—the Renaissance—and shone solarly with the inexpressible mystery of Raphael's paints.

That which flowed in paints from the frame of dogmatics was an action of the impulse of the Alexandrian ecstasies in man's blood; the migration of Plotinus from eastern Egypt to the west and to "Rome" was deeply symbolic. Plotinus was an inspirer of the poetry of the later "Rome" (in the Renaissance); he was a "Roman" philosopher; Alexandria mysteriously threw a bridge across the sea—into Italy.

It was Alexandria that illuminated Ravenna with glistening mosaic and poured her solar rays through the iron papacy, creating the *Civitas Solis* of Italy, the culture of art, "Raphael."

But an earlier frame of her solar disk was the bronze shield and the sword of the heavy Roman warrior—a distorted hint at the ray of Italy's life.

19

In later Europe we clearly see the intercrossing of cultures.

One line is the line of rational thought: from Greece—to France; from the classical drama to an uncomprehended "pseudo-classical" culture of the arts; from democracy and the republican order to new efforts to create a democratic life, to the "commune." And then one clearly sees the line: Alexandria—Italy (Rome, the Renaissance). This line is further highlighted by the flow of the paints of Italy—to Dürer; of the thought of Italy to the mountain range of the new "Germanic" systems of philosophy; of the "sword" and "shield" to the Prussian helmet. Alexandria, having flowed into Italy in the *paints* of Plotinus' ecstasy and in the *light* of Paul's "Vision," flows over into Germany in Bach's music; but above the channel of Germany's philosophies, poetries, and musics, containing the secret sun of a fallen culture, there arises a frame that shifts all the perspectives: the pan-German.

The pan-German is a product of imperialism; Zarathustra's superman is the product of a mysterious impulse of the sun. The religious antinomy of Alexandrian culture (Christ or Caesar) has now been replaced in Germany by the cultural antinomy of Nietzsche and Bismarck.

Alexandrian solarness, "music," the unrepeatable *Faust*—all this materialized in the unique, in Nietzsche. The *imperium*, the shield, the helmet, Kant's lash (the categorical imperative, or "*eiserne Handschuh*")[28]—all this materialized in Bismarck; and Bismarck opposes Nietzsche as the terrifying double of his aspirations.

Imperialism, law, the "lash"—all this is the same dwarf of doubts, the same Mime the Nibelung[29] whom Nietzsche always hated, against whom he struggled, and at whose hand he perished.

20

Germany's culture flows down from the heights of the Italian Renaissance through Bach; the fugue flying down from above (from the angels) sang the *hierarchy* of Alexandrian symbolism. Bach is the same for music as Dante is for poetry; both are rays of the Alexandrian sun. Meanwhile, Beethoven is a reflection of heaven in the boiling foam of the rebellious blood; superheated by the sun that has fallen into it, it boils like a rebellion.

The further path of culture consisted in a regeneration of the blood, where the blood grew wings to fly; the blood became like a cloud. The rebellion of Romanticism, individuality and its growth—these were spring storms thawing the ice, before the clarity of summer.

But we carry these storms within ourselves as the tragedy of a dying person who is destined to become an individual, a man, freedom.

Two were filled with the torment of tragedy: Schumann and Schubert.

28. "Iron glove."
29. A character in Wagner's Ring Cycle.

21

The significance of the song cycles is insufficiently seen; as in the case of the "Madonna" of Italy and Leonardo's "Christ," we are confronted with the incomprehensible song cycle *Winterreise*. Franz Schubert goes ahead of us like an uncomprehended wanderer; behind him is rebellion; and he, like Saul and like "Zarathustra," fractured with musical sounds the form of the unitary "symphony." It is all in song splashes, but out of the "mosaic" of songs a path is formed: he who has the gift of sound will hear that this is the "path to Damascus," the path to the vision, the path to Leonardo's "Last Supper" under a bright night: in the winter the midnight sun burns above you.

From the "feast" of the past to the mystery of the future "Last Supper" through the desolate winter—that is the path to the culture that is to come. The abandoned feast is the Renaissance, earthly spring and earthly love.

The *niveau* of *Winterreise* is not understood; its pedestal is the cycle of the unrepeatable Schumann, *Dichterliebe*,[30] where the lyrical intensity of love, exploding into tragedy, kills the utterly shattered earthy personhood; and "giants" of passion bury the latter.

At the peak of love we find death and night; from the peak through the coldness of the spaces begins the path of *Winterreise*—the after-death pilgrimage of the wanderer, or the *via dolorosa* of the soul.

In truth: if one has traced in his spirit the connection of the song cycles and understood that from *Dichterliebe* follows *Winterreise*, then he has understood the unique path: the path from the man of Italy to the man concealed in us beneath the cold scabs of our contemporary frozen culture, the path to... the Guest who is to come mysteriously into our hearts.

We traverse a landscape vivified by a raven's cries. We hear the cries of the culture or of the "raven" in Stirner's "Unique One"; in Kierkegaard, "the unhappiest of men"; in the "vilest" poem of the new period, *Thus Spoke Zarathustra*.

Zarathustra, too, is a wanderer. Listening to the chilling sounds of one song from *Winterreise*, *Die Krähe* ("The Raven"), we know per-

30. Set to the words of Heine. (Bely's note)

fectly well that this bird, circling, is not a crow, but an initiatory raven; we know that the "raven" was a stage of the initiation into the ancient Persian mysteries. The raven is our personal "I," pecking in us; it is our spirit. To see the "raven" or to stand above the "raven" is to uncover the "person" in oneself and to die to personal life. We know that initiation is the mystery of tragedy and that life is the mystery of death. And, listening to the sounds of *Die Krähe*, we see the mystery of the solitary Zarathustra, wandering from east to west and suddenly turning to himself:

Ein Krähe war mit mir
Aus der Stadt gezogen.[31]

The raven's sinister shadow stretches forth from the "city" of dying culture, obscuring the spaces of the spiritual world. We see this shadow.

This is the extreme of solitude; this is the final mountain-ledge between the human person and the "man" living secretly in the person. One cannot arrive at the "man" in oneself without dying: that which kills us we truly see as the attacking "raven."

The line of the person, the line of time within us, makes a circle: like a snake, it bites its own tail.

22

In Schubert's musical structure we find the solar light of Raphael's form; individual notes are just dabs of the brush, but their gradation is a perfect scale of nuances.

Thus, the *Winterreise* cycle is permeated by form as by a secret and invisible solar city. Here, the "*Civitas Solis*" is in the middle of "I" and within "I." All the edges of "I" (or of the "person") are ripped apart; in them, the "I" of passions has died for the "I" of life.

Listening to *Winterreise*, we feel that we have lost our ground and that we must build something in places where there is nothing. Descent, the dead night, is before us; winter, the cries of the raven; and our path lies through the dead street of the dead city.

31. "A raven has been following me ever since I left the city."

Eine Straße muß ich gehen,
Die noch keiner ging zurück.[32]

Nevertheless, in the dying of the wanderer we hear a call: in this song, in *Der Wegweiser*, suddenly we mysteriously hear a Bach chorale; and into the despair of our *winter wandering* there again breaks a sound signifying Zarathustra's sun, Paul's "Vision," Plotinus' "ecstasies," St. Francis' little flowers, and the musical currents of Augustine's soul.

Something tells us:

Die Sonne schaue
Um mitternächtige Stunde.
Mit Steinen baue
Im lebenlosen Grunde.

So finde im Niedergang
Und in des Todes Nacht
Der Schöpfung neuen Anfang,
Des Morgens junge Macht.[33]

23

The creative activity of the new day begins with torments, with the terror of descent; in this turning of attention on ourselves, we are visited by death.

Eine Straße muß ich gehen,
Die noch keiner ging zurück.

This Straße is the path of descent of Schumann and of Nietzsche—into madness. The midnight remains unrecognized here. "Mitternacht" sounds; it is the unrecognized path of initiation; Zarathustra's shadow is the dwarf that has crept up to him; and when Zarathustra, or the wanderer, sees the dwarf, he shudders: "It is not the heights that

32. "I must follow a street of no return." (From *Der Wegweiser*)

33. "The sun shines in midnight hours on stone buildings on lifeless ground. In descent and in the dead night, find the new beginning of creation and the young power of the morning." (From a poem by Rudolf Steiner)

frighten us, but the way down."[34] Midnight entered Nietzsche's consciousness as the falsehood of *repeatability.*

The dwarf struck down Zarathustra:

"O Zarathustra," he whispered distinctly, "you threw yourself high into the air, but every stone that is thrown must fall."

"O Zarathustra, you have condemned yourself to be slain by stoning: you have thrown your stone high, but it will fall on you."

The dwarf added:

"Everything that is straight is false... All truth is bent; time itself is a circle."

Rectilinear motion is half false, but it is also half true.

The path in *Winterreise* is linear and full of bad infinity: the raven's cry proclaims the infinity of wandering, the infinity of suffering, the solitude of "I."

> Eine Straße muß ich gehen,
> Die noch keiner ging zurück.

24

We think by contrasts.

The line fills us with the thought of the circle, and the path of no return leads to our return. But both the line and the circle are false.

Truth is found in spiral motion.

The dwarf exposed the falsehood of linear motion and caught Zarathustra in the falsehood of the circle. He incited Zarathustra with the idea of eternal return, and against his will Zarathustra yielded to the dwarf's cunning incitement:

"All that runs, has it not already run on this road? All the things that can happen, have they not already happened?"[35]

Afterwards, Zarathustra leaves the mountains and descends to the sea; the mountains inspire luminous reflection, the sea is associated with the seething of images. Thus, Zarathustra's return can be likened to a fall from the mountains.

34. From *Thus Spoke Zarathustra.*
35. Ibid.

The assertion of repetition is the turning of Zarathustra toward Zarathustra's shadow. Zarathustra's *wandering* echoes the great Schubert's song cycle; and the end of *Winterreise* rises; *Winterreise* ends with the meeting with the organ-grinder; this is a strange old man (perhaps the "Eternal Jew"); he cranks the barrel organ.

Where this eternal organ-grinder rose, is it not there that linear evolution transitions into circles? Circular motion spins and *whirls*, and the vertigo, the *vertige*, begins precisely here.

It is here that madness falls on Friedrich Nietzsche.

25

The flow-channels of culture end here. On these channels, life-giving water has flowed from the 2nd and 1st centuries to the 20th century. But now their source is drying up and we must turn once again and understand the *impulse* in ourselves. In the superman we must come to know man, who is the fusion of his doubles (of Kant and Faustus the Manichean teacher); we must unite two paths, the linear path and the path of the fixed circle, into a spiral.

In our own *Winterreise* we must come to understand that there is no more motion forward, just as there is no more dogma. We realize that there is a *reincarnation* of the impulses: in Schubert we recognize the reincarnated Bach; In Bach we hear the sounds of Augustine's life; in the sounds of the *Confessions* we recognize reflections of the luminous image on the way to our own Damascus.

To understand this image is to understand the impulse of the new culture.

26

But Nietzsche did not understand it. When he met the "raven" of the initiation, Nietzsche did not overpower him; he did not become the "raven." Instead, the "raven" pecked apart Nietzsche's brain with the winter cry of *eternal return*; fleeing from Basel, he could say:

Ein Krähe war mit mir
Aus der Stadt gezogen.

And, like the wanderer from Schubert's *winter wandering*, perhaps he exclaimed before his madness:

Krähe wunderliches Tier![36]

The Krähe attacks wanderers in Basel with his cry; I too have heard his voice. In Basel, often "the prisoner becomes madness! Through madness . . . the captive will frees itself."[37]

This was suggested to me by my stay in Basel: my winter wandering, my *Winterreise*, started there. My *captive will* was freeing itself from the fetters that had enchained me in Russia; near Basel I met Zarathustra's shadow; and there the raven's cry was directed at me. Not long before, I had fled Basel into the mountains, and then:

Ein Krähe war mit mir
Aus der Stadt gezogen.

27

Our life is a dead Basel from which we flee into the mountains (the Johannes Building is still unfinished). Chasing us, the "ravens" attack us with their cry: "Stop, turn around." Turning around, we see the treacherous way down; our shadow lies there, upside down; it seems to us that we are falling; prudence creeps into our soul, and we return to Basel.

Our *return* is like falling into an abyss.

Return to the impulses of the Renaissance is the promise that a new culture will be born; return to its feasts and forms is a fall and death. The Renaissance gave us a cosmos but, in the process of its creation, every cosmos is minted out of musically singing chaos; the cosmos is an oleograph; to repeat the forms of the Renaissance is to trample on its testaments.

The impulses of the Renaissance can be found in Alexandria; and, before that, they poured onto the earth in the Vision of the Luminous

36. "The raven is a wondrous animal!"
37. From *Thus Spoke Zarathustra*.

Light, in Paul's vision; and to repeat the forms of the Renaissance is to shut us off from the summoning Light—by the frame and shield.

To all the luxuries of life, to all the comforts of culture we must say our "no." We must flee from them into the mountains; we must depart on our *winter wandering*, undergo the appearance of the Krähe, and descend into the dead street of the dead city about which the wanderer's voice told us:

> Eine Straße muß ich gehen,
> Die noch keiner ging zurück.

28

Our gaze contemplates a desolation of abomination. We defend the ascent of our attainment against the abomination; our path is not yet finished (or even begun), but we have no time to think about that: the desolation, like a boa constrictor, directs its hypnotic gaze at us. We fly like little birds into the mouth of the snake, even though we think we are *attacking* it; that is perhaps what a little bird thinks when it flies straight into a snake's mouth.

Return to the values of contemporary culture results from our fear of the *agonizing winter wandering*. The *Winterreise*, as the path of initiation into Leonardo's "Last Supper," fills us full of fear. Meanwhile, the coziness of our cabinet and the piece of pie on the table, protected by the state, seem to us not a *desolation of abomination* but *comforts of culture*; and having read in comfort about the wanderings of Wilhelm Meister, we return—to our four walls, and the "cube" of our cabinet, heated by steam, seems to us the peak of culture.

But the "cube" of the cabinet is a "prison."

Return into one's "own" cabinet is an upside-down return; and the meaning of the cabinet is an *upside-down meaning*: you keep telling yourself that childish amusements with dreams have resulted in the epoch of *the evaluation of transvaluations by the transvaluation of evaluations*.

Between "e" and "trans" lies an abyss; to gallop over prefixes is more perilous than people think (prefixes are steep). A universally inapplicable verbless insubstantiality—that is what a *prefix* is; and the *prefix* of the return into the coziness of state-protected cabinets of culture is unique; it is a universally inapplicable preoccupation with *insubstantiality*, with the systematics of catalogues of museum relics of culture. As opposed to creative activity, systematics generates here a catalogue of catalogues (nomenclature and terms): the nomenclature of terms is the keyboard of a piano on which we touch key after key, extracting pleasant sounds: "tam-tam—Raphael; tam-tam-tam—Leonardo; tam—Wagner; ta-ta-tam—Friedrich Nietzsche."

We pleasantly spend our time extracting these sounds of culture without considering that the sounds are extracted into the idleness of the path; the scale of sounds of the piano of culture with which we are amusing ourselves is tantamount to an infatuation with a series of crosses and crowns of thorns: our condition at the feast of culture can be likened to the viewing of a gladiatorial contest. The fingering of the keys of the instrument (the piano of culture) is sentimental to the extreme. Sentimentality is a hidden form—of monstrous, super-sensual impulses.

The return to culture by going into the "cube" of the cabinet is a sensual game that does not lead to anything good.

A quiet evening and the sounds of a piano and a voice singing "*Die Krähe*." Madman, listen to how your heart beats! Do you sleep at night? You will answer: "no."

Are you still sleeping?

You will awaken: the floor of the cabinet will cave in; in your armchair you will be suspended over the abysses of night. There will be a moon: an attacking, engorged, stony globe flying straight at you. That will be an illusion. You'll fall into the abyss, and the house out of which you fell will hang idly above you like an empty shell. Prudence, having returned you into the "cube" of culture (into the domestic coziness), returned you there in order to—cast you down precipitously: instead of going voluntarily, like the wanderer, into the winter (through the winter) toward the mysteriously hidden Sun, you, having prudently prepared warm clothing, will be cast down into that coldness by force without the possibility of arming yourself against the accidents of the wandering.

29

We did not see a desolation of abomination in the middle of the "cube" of culture given to us: "when ye shall see the abomination of desolation . . . standing where it ought not . . . let them that be in Judaea flee to the mountains. . . . And let him that is on the housetop not go down into the house. . . . And let him that is in the field not turn back again. . . ." (Mark 13:14). But all of us turn back, and our turning back to the abomination is the beginning of our repetition in it.

Standing guard with a sword is not the way to defend the ideals of culture bequeathed by Nietzsche; nor can they be defended by attacking what is lower (attacking Reger proves nothing about Beethoven, and distorting anything at all in an effort to glorify Goethe does not reveal the worth of Goethe). No, we defeat that which is lower by ascending above it. If we try to fight the windmills of *circular motion*, we will end up in Don Quixote's position: on our wings we will describe a complete circle and smash down against the stone from which we had ascended in the same way that Nietzsche smashed down against his *eternal repetition*: he began life as a hero and ended it as a Don Quixote.

Let us recall: the first news of the return begins with Nietzsche's cry: "On your feet, you, thought that makes my head spin and that has come out of the depths of my being."[38] A strange note of merriment possesses the solitary wanderer, Zarathustra. This strange note of merriment also possesses another wanderer dear to us, the wanderer of *Winterreise*—when he meets the organ-grinder. This strange organ-grinder, whom we flee without listening to him and without giving any money to him, is the temptation of return; he stands exactly where the turning toward ourselves begins on our path, the turning of Zarathustra toward the shadow! "It is not the heights that frighten us, but the way down" . . . "Time itself is a circle."[39]

Keiner mag ihn hören,
Keiner sieht ihn an...

38. From *Thus Spoke Zarathustra*.
39. Ibid.

Und sein kleiner Teller
Bleibt ihm immer leer.[40]

Having seen the strange old organ-grinder ("Time itself is a circle"), the wanderer exclaims:

Wunderlicher Alter!
Soll ich mit dir geh'n?
Willst zu meinen Liedern
Deine Leier dreh'n?[41]

Further, the *Winterreise* breaks off. What happens next? The madness of Zarathustra, who could not withstand the test of the *eternal* return and exclaimed like the Wanderer in the winter wandering: "Will you *turn* your barrel organ for my songs?"

Vertigo comes next: "On your feet, you, thought that makes my head spin. . . ."

He experiences the meeting with eternity as an *eternal* return; something in him distorts the call of eternity. This something is perhaps Nietzsche's *black* point—the experiencing of "I" not as an impersonal Individuum but as an engorged and enlarged person. "I am a sleeping dragon."[42]

This is that very same terrible Krähe—the *raven of consciousness* (the personal "I") which follows Nietzsche from Basel into the mountains:

Ein Krähe war mit mir
Aus der Stadt gezogen.

He could exclaim:

Krähe wunderliches Tier!

40. "No one likes to listen to him, no one likes to look at him. . . . And his little collection plate is always empty." (From *Winterreise*)

41. "Strange old man! Should I go with you? Will you turn your barrel organ for my songs?" (From *Winterreise*)

42. From *Thus Spoke Zarathustra*.

"The Krähe has returned," caws Nietzsche. "If you've returned, you were here before. If you here before, you will always be here."

There is nothing new under the moon.

And Zarathustra is in agony: "Go away... I feel revulsion!" This is followed by Nietzsche's *mute* silence, by his *quiet hour*. The *quiet hour* is repeated. Nietzsche himself becomes the quiet hour; after him, culture is nothing but a *quiet* hour—before all the buildings, the frames of culture, are blown up.

We thought the *quiet hour* was a pastorale of the cabinet but it is actually the intensification of atmospheric electricity before the storm with its thunder and lighting, destroying the comfortable cabinet...

30

Nietzsche is the leading edge of all culture; his leading edge is the meeting with the dwarf of the "return." Our infatuation with Nietzsche and Ibsen was genuine: for a single moment we desired to escape into the mountains. In the mountains we found ourselves moist and warm; columns of mist everywhere; a mist of soulness veiled the path of ascent to the spirit. *Strangenesses* pierced us (midway on the mountains—between the valleys and the mountain peaks—dwell cretins,[43] burned by the lightning of the spirit). We became cretins; in Nietzsche we saw not a body broken by the spirit but a literary form; and we began to imitate this form, grimacing with the symbol. Our chronic cretinism evolved into *Kulturträgerism*: every time we were called to risk our lives in the name of the tasks of the mountain peaks, we gave the callers' calls to the bookbinders—and so the "collected works" lay before us in their moiré bindings and the bindings crushed the calls of life.

31

Nietzsche is the dialogue between a God crying in the wilderness and a cretin. He is both God and "cretin"; Zarathustra speaks in imprints of strangeness: imagination is spiritualized in him to—the point of meeting the "organ-grinder" of the return. He questions the organ-grinder:

43. See note 2 on p. 105.

Wunderlicher Alter!
Soll ich mit dir geh'n?
Willst zu meinen Liedern
Deine Leier dreh'n?

The eagle of the spirit in him battles against the boa constrictor: against the snake of the return. The battle of the eagle and the serpent lasts for years; it has no end; the union of the serpent and the eagle is the *dragon*. Out of the depths of Nietzsche's personhood, at the threshold of the culture to come, grows the dragon: "I am a sleeping dragon."

The final landmarks of a once enormous culture rise before us in the form of madness, or the dragon; the impulse of life descends *into the hell* of our life in order to raise us to itself. The raising of the life of the previous impulse signifies the break of our life. The "cubic" cabinet with the *quiet hour* concealed in it is the grave and hell, the winter wandering of all human life. That is what Nietzsche's suffering signifies; he is crucified in his cabinet to which he had returned from the mountains after having gone only "mid-way" (after failing to reach the peak). Together with him, culture from the 1st to the 20th century had reached its limit.

The light that descended into the Crucified One, Paul, Plotinus, Augustine, Leonardo, the dual Faust, who split into Kant and Nietzsche (Kant represents "the cabinets of culture" and Nietzsche is the attempt to begin the ascent). Through the series of these persons (from Augustine to Nietzsche) there passes, permeating all of them, the invisibly hidden stream that constitutes the palette of colors and the gradation of fugues and cathedrals. This stream sings from Bach and sobs in Beethoven; in our own age it has disappeared into the depths, down to the hidden source in us, but this trapped stream is waiting to erupt out of us and to splash against the sky; it is waiting to turn into a spiral midway and, in alternations of linear and circular motion, to become our path and pilgrimage to the "Last Supper."

32

We have accepted Nietzsche and all his strangenesses as if they were the bacilli of sicknesses eating away at our brain. He could also be our yeast if we could understand that the circle and the line of culture are both false; both the "raven" of time and the "circle" of timelessness (the "organ-grinder") are temptations. The furious Friedrich attempted to overpower these temptations by inoculating himself with the poison of repetitions, but the inoculation didn't work and *repetition* overpowered Nietzsche. He was crushed by the heavy inertia of "culture," by the "cubic cabinet," by comfort, by "Kant."

Our salvation lies in playful exuberance, and the name of this exuberance is "the battle unto death." But, again, we replace it with surrogates, with the tarantellas of rational thought (the word "tarantella" derives from the sting of a tarantula). Who is the tarantula? Kant, of course. Kant!

We have learned playful exuberance from contemporary philosophy, which has hurled *purified* or *Kantian* reason (in which, let us note, almost nothing of Kant remains) into the abyss of *non-ontic meaning*. It flies upside down and the modernist-gnoseologist flies upside down after it, continuing to hold the revered "Critiques of . . . Reason" and reading them backwards, from right to left, so that one gets the nonsensical "Nosaer Erup fo Euqitirc" (instead of "Critique of Pure Reason").

But I suppose that "Nosaer," too, is a form of reason.

33

"Kant was an Idiot," Nietzsche said. But the "idiot" defeated the "sage": the climax of Kantianism is a theory grounding "circular motion" (let philosophers laugh!). The structure of the sentence "consciousness is the form of the form of consciousness" Kantianizes our view of consciousness as it is refracted in Lask's philosophy[44] (alas, Lask was killed in the war!). The modernism of philosophy is a circular motion; here, consciousness fructifies itself: consciousness is hermaphroditic; hermaphroditic is the "philo-sophist" of culture begotten from Lask and Cohen. Amidst the company of the "snobs, satyrs, and Eulenspiegels" of contemporary culture, he truly is not last in the ranks of these little demons, shaping and orienting them in "Kant." At the same

44. Allusion to Emil Lask (1875–1915), Neo-Kantian philosopher.

time, he has the look neither of a child nor of a grown-up man; he is rather a debauched youth who has tasted Nietzsche; his engorged brain, expanding, breaks through his skull, spilling out in all directions. Meanwhile, his body atrophies and this newly hatched "tarantulik," whirling on his feet, leaps at the galloping "satyrs" and flitting "Eulenspiegels"—the sons of billionaires, collectors, and bibliographers.

34

We did not go up into the heights but rolled down to "culture," out of the depths of which cannons are shooting at us. We have traded the madness of the mountains for "Kant" and "Krupp," first (for the sake of our comfort) having covered both of them with "paintings" of mountain landscapes.

We have traded the experience of ascent in ourselves for the experience of *the contemplation of the mountains* (or simply for the experience of sitting on verandahs of Swiss hotels). Instead of going up into the mountains, we went to a diorama, that is, to a diorama of the theater, where we saw a play by Ibsen. We saw the actor playing Rubek[45] striding on the wooden stage toward calico glaciers, to be flipped over by a white avalanche of pressed cotton. A displacement of reality was achieved by replacing oleographic decorations with triangles, cubes, and gesticulating 90-degree angles. The theater strode on these angles toward the glaciers; people were glued like frescos to the theater walls; and then, to roam among us, a stylized genius of culture descended from the stage; he was improbably simplified—in what was altogether unsimplifiable.

35

We followed Nietzsche to the heights of sweetest expectation, and we saw that Nietzsche perished. It seems there is only one thing left for us to do: to begin at the place where he ended, in the same way in which he ended (dying in relation to all that lay below) in order to end as he began.

45. Sculptor Arnold Rubek, character in *When We Dead Awaken*.

He began with *mystery*, and because he began with mystery, he could say: "I am a messenger who brings good news. . . . I know the tasks of a height for which . . . concepts had been absent; with me, hopes are born."[46]

Our task is to detect the impulse imparted by Nietzsche to culture and to remove from this impulse the veils of sensualism, of "scientism," and of the *irrationality* that rationally rejects thought. The tasks of Alexandria have not been understood, and the Renaissance has been simplified.

Having removed all these things that were veiling Nietzsche's consciousness, we see nothing but symbols. They nod silently at us—with a piercing impulse. Nietzsche summons us to doves and flowers;[47] *doves descend in clouds of love.*[48] The symbols shine with the sun, and the *Civitas Solis* descends into the heart. And he says now: "You hear without seeking" and "thought flares up like lightning, with necessity . . . without vacillation." Lifted up is an ancient gold goblet of "happiness where an abundance of light acts cruelly within."[49]

In other words, it is as if thoughts think themselves.

And such thoughts are streams from the source—from Nietzsche's impulse.

36

The state of the vivification and purification of thought constitutes the "nerve" of the *Enneads*. Starting with the problem of the soul and ascending to the purification of thought, Plotinus preaches the contemplation of the mental landscapes of the universe. The Orphic-Pythagorean school glistens transfiguratively in him—with the poetry of thought and with ecstasy. The line of thought is stretched taut here, and it produces its own sound like a string. Further, this string, suddenly melting, slithers like a bright snakelet from a life-giving source. Leaping from it, we fly into the landscapes of theories.

46. From *Ecce Homo.*
47. From *Thus Spoke Zarathustra.*
48. Ibid.
49. From *Ecce Homo.*

Rudolf Steiner, too, speaks of this state of thought:

> In deinem Denken leben Weltgedanken,
> In deinem Fühlen weben Weltenkräfte,
> In deinem Willen wirken Weltenwesen.[50]

It is in such a state of consciousness that Zarathustra came to Friedrich Nietzsche.

37

Here, near Basel, I remember the thoughts I had then, and those thoughts transport me to Christiania,[51] to Lian, where my wife[52] and I lived beneath the rays of the Norwegian sunsets, above a fjord, in the coziest of rooms. This room lacked a fourth wall; instead, a glass door opened out onto a little balcony hanging over the fjord, and the windows threw spaces of water into the overly illuminated room. The impression that it was only a boat never deserted me; I imagined the floor was made of two wooden boats bound together, that tables and armchairs were thrown onto the floor, and that we sat with feet curled up on the armchairs from morning till night immersed in our thoughts or in a variegated multiplicity of the drawings scattered around us. Spaces of turquoise air poured into the room through the two windows and the glass door; and it seemed that with its unenclosed side the room would suck in the turquoise air and we would be capsized (without having time to scream) and float out into clear space.

The Norwegian sunset, engulfing the surroundings, amazes me. A serene clarity transubstantiates the fjords; the movement of the air stretches the distances; a bright-pawed cloud hangs suspended; lemon-colored bands of moisture pour down, turn into mist, and disappear.

At times, wrapped in a cloak and wearing a high black-silhouetted

50. "In thy thoughts lives the thought of the world. In thy feelings weaves the power of the world. In thy will acts the essence of the world." (To Lina Schliephak-Utter, December 1910)

51. Old name for Oslo, Norway.

52. The artist Anna Alekseevna ("Asya") Turgeneva (1890–1966), Bely's first wife, was a leading anthroposophist and close collaborator of Rudolf Steiner.

hood, my wife, leaping from stone to stone, would descend to the waters—in order to eavesdrop on the chatter of the frightened streamlets splashing onto the stones. Squinting from the light, we observe the jellyfishes; an improbable sunset bursts into flame—and does not want to fade.

Our reflections to which we surrendered in Lian continued a line of thought that progressed over a series of months. Cities rushed past us: Munich, Basel, Vitznau. Galleries and museums opened themselves up to us from a distance: the severe Grünewald, Lucas Cranach with his brilliant colors, Dürer and Holbein the Younger—all of them threw to us the inexpressible thought of their palettes. We listened to the weeping dark green waves of Lake Lucerne, over which Wagner once reflected when he lived in Tribschen. Rudolf Steiner thundered at us with his lectures from Munich and Basel; and our sharp line of thought dug for us a well, carrying us into Strasbourg: we were burned by the "flamboyant" Gothic style. Nuremberg flew past; above Stuttgart we heard the noisy pines in mute Degerloch; Cologne and Berlin rushed past; Paul's Epistles and the wondrous "Gita" opened themselves up to us from Helsingfors and Cologne; from Dresden the Madonna gazed at us and then—we arrived in Christiania and Lian.

The places changed, but their unchanging center remained: the labor of thought.

38

Displacements of consciousness visited us, and our thoughts thought themselves. And in my thought-streams arose the thought-streams of my wife, Asya. She frequented the core of my thoughts, and we recognized each other—in each other; and with schemata of utterly inexpressible states of consciousness we penetrated into each other down to the deepest depths. Asya's thought-images became for me soul-beings who visited me, and in her album I saw that she had drawn all my thought-images: a crucified dove woven of light, a hexagram, wings without heads and a winged crystal, a spiral ornament (the beating of an etheric body), and a chalice (or was it a gorge-Grail?); and I know that these drawings were only symbols of the thought-rhythms of the life-impulse that cut through both of us.

39

I'd sit down in a comfortable armchair on the little terrace hanging over the pines, the strata of stones, and the fjord; and I'd concentrate all my attention on the thoughts that were sucking into themselves my feelings and impulses. My body, covered with rhythms of thought, did not hear the inertia of its organs; some clear thing within me was flying through my skull into vastnesses; it zestfully propelled itself by rhythms as if by wings (winged images are rhythms: the arrangement, shape, and number of angels' wings are eurhythmic). I was multi-winged; sparks were shooting out of my eyes and weaving themselves together; the weaving of the sparks created images for me; and the crucified dove woven of light, the headless wings, and the winged crystal, twisting themselves into spirals, were untwisted spirally (how I loved the spiral ornament in Asya's album!). Once I saw a sign: a triangle composed of lightnings, placed on an ultra-luminous crystal and emitting cosmoses of light; and within it there was an "eye" (you'll see this sign in one of Jacob Boehme's books).

All my thoughts, becoming compressed, were formed as a spiral: being transported, I was drilling through the spaces of an elemental sea. If I had lifted up my head at that moment, I would have seen not the azure of the heavens, but a dread black breach with coldness ripping apart my body and sucking me, a dying man, into unbelievable torments. I would have understood that this breach into *nowhere and nothing* is a window into the truth—into the world beyond the grave. It would ignite for me with effulgent azure lights (I had seen an azure sphere in Asya's album), pulling me through itself, and I would have flown out of my head, rising like noisy steam through the opening of a samovar's pipe. I would become a multi-eyed sphere gazing at a point in the middle; and feeling this point with my hands, I would sense, as if it were coldness, my trembling skin; and my body would be like the pit of a juicy peach. I—skinless and diffused into everything—would feel myself to be a zodiac.

(The zodiac drawings in Asya's album had convinced me that our work was guiding us on the same path.)

I would be scattered into a swarm of star-eyed beings: the resonant swarm would be contained within me and I would be the spirit of this swarm of star-bees. My golden bees would fly down to a point expanding into the dome of my corporeal temple (or hive); and I would know, flying with the whole swarm through an opening in the dome (or through an opening in my skull), that my thoughts were no longer thinking me and that the meditation had ended.

The terrace together with the top of a pine re-appeared before me; I turned my head toward Asya. I saw her: she looked like a taut little string in a white dress, with her eyes glistening in such a way as to illuminate her whole face and pour the brightness of health into her whole being. She laughed joyously and took my hand, and we went out for a stroll. Squinting from the light and leaping from stone to stone, we rushed down to the fjord to look at the splashing of the waves and admire the jellyfishes.

In swarms of transparent star-bees we merged into a single starry apiary, being transported into the sphere of thought; and then we flew apart again—toward the domes of our abandoned corporeal temples. We knew we were called to work on temples, with the toil of our thought cutting majestic treasure-houses of canons of conscious life out of the wood of sensuous impulses; I knew that Asya, when in my temple, labored over me with a heavy hammer and a chisel, cutting out in my being those super-strange forms of *remembrances of my pre-natal country* which later constituted my *Kotik Letaev*.[53]

Later we worked in Dornach on the wooden forms of the dancing architraves and giant portals of the Johannes Building: Armed with a chisel and cutting off fragrant shavings from heavy American oak which had the distinct odor of almond or apple (due to the presence in the wood of aromatic benzyl esters), in the gradation of the planes composing the forms and in the gradation of my thought-rhythms, I recognized the land of living thought. Asya and I sojourned in this land, performing labors of thought in Lian; and the dome of the Johannes Building became for me the symbol of the dome of my *theoretical* journeys, of the materialization of the thought-flights constituting the building of the new culture.

That's what culture is in fact: the crystallization of living rhythms of

53. Autobiographical novel by Bely (1917–18).

soarings of self-thinking thought; only later do its arabesques, its spirals, materialize in simple forms—in circular or rectilinear motions.

And theories emerge—of the lines of culture; and theories emerge—of the planar circles of culture.

But the source of thought contains not abstract schemata but clear and living arabesques; the *spiral* is the simplest line of thought-flight; but rational thought utterly lacks a theory of spirally growing cultures; the theory of the reincarnation of primordially posited thought in the Kulturträgers' theories splits apart into a theory of evolution and a theory of dogma.

40

The eternal succession of *instants* and life *in an instant* are the line of evolution; and the philosophy of the "instant" stretches as a line in the latter. The decadent, the preacher of the instant, defends himself, in essence, by means of Herbert Spencer.

The *circle* negates the instant; the philosophy of *lines* biting their own tails is dogmatism: evolution is folded up into a circle of thought. And in dogma we have the eternal return of instants; in motion forward it bears no fruit. There is nothing new under the moon.

The truth of the spiral unites *circle with line*. The union of the three motions consists in the ability to control all the modes of the motion of one's thought. The culture we yearn for is given in two projections: in parallels of smokestacks that spew soot into our sky; and in circles of state-regulated horizons that constrict our creative acts.

The Areopagite sketched three motions of thought: *straight*, leading us to supra-sensuous thought; and *spiral* and *circular*. The latter, culminating in ecstasies, is shackled in dogmas.

These wheels of thought are not allegories but the images of rhythms; the degrees of hierarchical life were called "minds" by the fathers: "For this reason in our priestly tradition the first minds are called light-giving forces."[54]

Rudolf Steiner says: "With regard to entities that attain degrees of being in the spiritual world . . . human beings feel that these entities

54. From *On the Celestial Hierarchy.*

consist wholly of the substance of thought...that they live in the fabric of thought. . . . And this thought-being of theirs has a back-effect on the world. Thoughts that are entities carry on conversations with other thoughts that are entities."[55]

The formation of rhythms, of wheels, is an attempt to represent the supra-sensuousness of thought in the material of the senses: "The formations in spiritually experienced people are called wheels (chakras) as well as 'lotus flowers.' They are called this because they resemble wheels and flowers. When a pupil begins his exercises, they begin to rotate."[56] "It is possible to see that there are wheels. . . . It is possible to interpret the description of the intelligent wheels. . . ."[57] "Now as I beheld the living creatures, behold one wheel upon the earth by the living creatures, with his four faces. The appearance of the wheels and their work was like unto the colour of a beryl: and they four had one likeness: and their appearance and their work was as it were a wheel in the middle of a wheel. . . . As for their rings, they were so high that they were dreadful; and their rings were full of eyes round about them four."[58]

> A flash of light in the darkness:
> All was remembered, without any questions.
> My molten soul flowed
> *Into boiling wheels.*

41

That which is written in the eternal books is truth and life, and therefore all the eternal books are not books but creations woven of sparks; the visible world itself is only the heart of some entity thrown from universe to universe.

A book is an entity; transecting three-dimensionality, the fourth dimension of the book forms the cube of the book, or the book *in octavo*; the page is a plane, the line is of course a line.

55. From *The Threshold of the Spiritual World.*
56. From Rudolf Steiner's *Path of Initiation.*
57. From *On the Celestial Hierarchy.*
58. From Ezekiel 1.

In reading, we effect motion: In transposing a line, we almost form with the motion of our eyes a complete circle. In joining page to page, we draw spirals: a true book is spiral in character: it is the constant change of that which remains unchanging; its truth is the reincarnation of what is unchanging in it.

If the line of evolution were able to actualize life, there would be no books: as long as you keep writing, everything's changed in you. If the world were dominated by the circle, then books would have been created before the creation of the world. There'd be nothing to write: all written things would have the form of a plane, and a plane is a circle. Books are possible only in a spiral, in the reincarnation of the once written book—of Destinies.

42

The soul of time is a unity of a self-conscious center. This center is our "I"; the soul of the lines on the page is a unity of self-constructing thought (our thought is constructed in us). The lines are first in the thought of corporeality; they are the first fiber enveloping the electric current of a brain shock. In the shocks we have the pulsations of the lines; the lines impact against objects, and the body of the glimmering lines is the page, which weaves together all the lines (the bones are constructed out of the connecting tissue). The sum of the pages is the mass of the muscles, and the title page is the skin. Thus, a book is the last enveloping in flesh of a living creation and the projection in three dimensions of a four-dimensional entity.

A book is a luminous Archangel crucified for our sake in the inert chaos of matter.

But books aren't read...

Read and listen: Here is the shock of the primordial creation. Commune with the archangelic thought, for the nation prophesies in the book. You will become the nation, expanding toward your motherland; a yard from yourself in all directions you will feel strange pulses outlining your profile and flashing gold and blue sparks in all directions; you will feel that you are going into the earth, beneath the earth, and through the earth. And you will feel that you are growing through the sky; and the sparks of the heavenly vault, pulsating, will spread over your chest. Your heaven and earth are within the being of your life; they are actively embraced by thought.

Who has risen there—immense, enormous, shining? You're outside yourself—with Yourself.

Everyday thought is the strong-boned skeleton of the first solar thought, which has thrown everyday feeling through the head of the thought: the feeling is the feeling of space, and the space constitutes the muscles of the solar creation. Will is now thrown into the heights through the muscles of the feelings, for will is time, and time constitutes nothing more than the nerves of our thought-entities. Will is the stream of blood of the universe.

Now you are only the sun that has illuminated the page—the sun that is inscribed in you from chest to head.

When you're reading books, you're outside yourself—with yourself.

43

Therefore the words about "wheels," "circles," "pentagrams," "spirals," and "lines" of thought are words about the super-immense truth of entities dwelling even in the schemata of rational thought. When you quicken this thought, you will say with Steiner: "These entities dwell in the fabric of thought. They consist of the substance of thought." The communications of thought evolve into eternally authentic life: the worlds of images are materializations of imageless thought, and the objects of reality are materializations of fantasy. If thought is pure air, then image is a cloud formed from the condensation of air into water vapor; and fantasy is therefore the condensation of the air of thought into the head: the nature that surrounds us is the crystallization of the moisture of fantasy. The world of fantasy rises in us not in the image and likeness of the nature that surrounds us, but in the image and likeness of the condensed thought; and that is why inspiration is the creativeness of the world.

Nietzsche is right: "The instinct of rhythmic relations . . . is almost the measure of the power of inspiration. . . . All things occur with a high degree of spontaneity, as if in a stream. . . . The powers, divinity, and spontaneity of a Symbol are what is most remarkable. . . . It truly appears . . . as if things come and offer themselves."[59] These are Nietzsche's "symbols." They are the composition of the first fruits of the future nature in the nature of fantasy; and out of the symbols the world is then formed. The essence of symbolism lies in the construction of the world; therefore, culture is always symbolic.

The crises of contemporary culture consist in the mixing of civilization and culture. Civilization is an artifact created from what is naturally given to us: that which has solidified and grown fixed and petrified in its forms becomes in civilization a material for production (thus from steel we can artificially produce knives). Culture is the formation of the material of steel from an image descending upon us from thought; civilization is always evolutive; culture is involutive; in culture out of thought-entities, out of the land of the life of thought, there pours into our soul something that comes to life there as an image that at some point descends in its explicit nature. An image is a symbol. It is thought-imbued; in other words, it is *alive*; thought is a living sun shining with a multitude of beams, rays, or "minds," as the Areopagite says. They are the entities of the hierarchical life: Archangels, Angels, Powers, Principalities, Dominions, and Thrones. All the images in us (or in culture) are the flesh of the life of these "minds"; natural images constitute the hair growing out of the sensuous body.

44

The lily, iris, and moon remind me of the Angel. The flame, sword, and poppy remind me of the archangel. The Principality whirls before me in the blue chrysanthemum; the flowery Powers are symbolized by the white rose, and the Spirit of Wisdom by the Bluebell.

Symbols form the nature of the soul, in order at some point to form through the soul a different nature. The continents on which we'll walk will turn into water and then into air; and the cultures we've outlived decompose into the world of natural objects and the world of abstract concepts. The latter, superimposed on the former, transforms it into a world of artifacts; culture is fantastic, and fantasy is woven of our thoughts; civilization is always factory-like.

59. From *Ecce Homo.*

The circle is the symbol of that which exists; the incarnation in time of that which exists is at present impossible. Civilization is a line constricting our horizon; our life is one-dimensional; in the culture which we await we'll see the union of *lines and circles in the spiral of symbolism.*

45

The line is a succession of instants and life in an instant; truth resides only in the last instant, but it is the combination of that which has been experienced in time. In the last instant we feel the whole line of time; it seems to us that we have risen above time and are riding on time; all the timelessnesses in an instant are an illusion; the sensation of speed is not Eternity.

"Evolution" is an artifact produced by many highly respected "eggheads," whereas the cult of the instant is artifact that sprang out of the heads of decadents. A doubt in the direction of the eggheads: "Can it be that the respected philosophy of Herbert Spencer is decomposing into decadence?" And a doubt in the direction of the decadents: they have sunk in the highly respected Herbert Spencer; evolutionary philosophy has engendered cubism and futurism, where the last instants of the arts are nothing but chaoses of the first instant (of prehistoric screams); the instant has been flattened into a complete circle and the line describes only a circle.

The law of evolution is that, progressing, it constantly deviates from the line—to the left; and it transforms progresses into regress; evolution transforms into nothing but the eternal return of the instant. In evolution the straight line is the line of a circle whose radius is infinity; the circle is dogma.

And the philosophy of evolution is ripped apart into dogmatism.

46

The instant is negated by the circle: that which is experienced is only a small segment of the path. Experience would be truth only if the present and future instants were contained in it *implicite*; their combination, having returned to the source, would not be poured into a line (the eternal is extratemporal: it exists in immobility); thought is immobile and its immobility is dogmatism.

The diversity of dogmatic truths in time has drawn over the centuries *the line of evolution* (*of dogmas*).

The "instant" of evolution is blown up from a frog into a cow: Cohen[60] is a Spencer who has burst; together with Spencer, who burst in Kant, all the futurists must burst in the canonical figures of creativity. The futuristic culture of the arts is the canon.

The ideal of the futurists is not form but the caprices of the neurasthenic "instant," whereas the ideal of the canonist is form (the Venus de Milo). Is form independent of "instants"? Is caprice formless?

Truly, the form of caprice is a point in the circle of dogma.

The philosophy of dogmatism keeps affirming the absence of meaning in time; evolution presupposes both time and the *line* of time. Meanwhile, there is no time in the *circle*; but, alas, the affirmation of the absence of time contains a "psychological" instant—this plebeian of philosophy: In a particular period of the history of philosophy the latter placed itself outside the laws of history; philosophy's historical lawlessness was historically legitimized; the only thing permitted it was *self-destruction*.

And philosophy became "psychology," the instant, a nervous tic, a convulsion, an agony, and . . . a difficulty. All of modern logism is a psychology of difficulty.

Dogma is no longer dogma if it "exists" and if this "exists" exists. This "exists" contains the beating instant such that the dogma is not a circle but a circle with a point. What connects the circle with the point? A spiral.

47

The symbol is a measurement of dogma, its *third* depth, for in the symbol dogma is not a circle but a spirally constructed cone of revolution. The line of evolution in the cone of the *dogma-symbol* is a plane (growing from a unique first-posited point) of circles and figures inscribed in a circle; all the points of all the lines of the figures and circles, flowing

60. Hermann Cohen (1842–1918), leading figure of Neo-Kantianism.

in time, expand; the original apex of the growing cone represents the union of the instant of Eternity; light fills the whole cone and chases and broadens, rotating, the traveling, growing, revealed dogma—in the incarnations of time.

Symbolism is the deepest depth of dogmatism and the growth of dogmatic truths. When it is thrown upside down into dogmatism, it is flattened, and when it is thrown upside down into evolution, it is narrowed and becomes a line. Dogmas from which linear time has dried up are "circles of width," but all that is planar widens; and the "synthetism" of dogmatic philosophies is a planar width, whereas the philosophy of evolution is a narrowness of bad infinity; the intersection of dogmas is a line; philosophers' debates, intersecting the circles of dogmatic truths, have crushed the dogmas of the philosophy of recent centuries into the evolutionary line of Spencer's philosophy, which constitutes a dust of dogmatic truths fragmented into aphorisms about the instant: the decadent's sophism is the crown of this philosophy.

The instant of dogma is the pulse of turnings of no return: dogmas of transformation, rotating, merge into dogmas of symbolism: in them we see the reincarnation of a once-posited truth which grows from point to cone. Man is the point as well as the circle, as well as the point in the circle. But the circle or sphere is the "world"; the world and "I," I and the "world," *are one* in the symbolic dogma; science proclaims the same thing about spirit.

And in us triangles are inscribed in the head, in the heart, and in the hands. We carry, move, and change their rhythms in ourselves; one being transformed into the circle of the others and turning toward this circle, feeling, will, and mind multiply our capabilities.

48

Two distortions of symbolism are encountered in the Luciferian temptation of philosophical dogmatism, in Ahrimanic evolution; we must crucify falsehood twice into ourselves in order to have two visions: of the crucified Ahriman and Lucifer.

These are the two visions before the "Vision" on the way to our Damascus. We have had the first; the second is coming; the third will come.

49

The Dionysianism of pure thought was not understood by Nietzsche: he did not understand Alexandria and had a frivolous view of the Renaissance.

By removing all this from Nietzsche's consciousness, we uncover symbols about which he said: "they nod silently to us without words."With what do symbols nod silently? With a radiant impulse: Nietzsche summons us—to doves and to flowers. Doves of the Spirit descend in a trembling cloud of love; these symbols shine with the sun and the solar city descends into the heart.

Our rejection of the Vision on the way to our Damascus deepens the Vision that has risen in the heart. Nietzsche's consciousness is separated by the namelessness in him of the singing impulse: in his unilluminated wandering there rose for him by instants the midnight sun; his song merges with St. Francis' hymn to the sun.

> "Ich schlief, ich schlief—,
> Aus tiefem Traum bin ich erwacht:—
> Die Welt ist tief,
> Und tiefer als der Tag gedacht.
> Tief ist ihr Weh—,
> Lust—tiefer noch als Herzeleid:
> Weh spricht: Vergeh!
> Doch alle Lust will Ewigkeit—,
> —will tiefe, tiefe Ewigkeit!"[61]

And truly: the eternity of joy is the joy of eternity. Nietzsche's song is interwoven here with Francis' all-joyous hymn.

Yes, Zarathustra's sun has been ripped apart; his secret is that his sun veils the Countenance, the Name: the unique Light is not visible to his eyes (only the surface of the shining is visible); the Sun veils the living countenance.

61. "I lay asleep, asleep—I waked from my deep dream. The world is deep, and deeper than even day may think. Deep is its woe—Joy— deeper than the heart's agony: Saith woe: Hence! Go! Yet joy wants eternity—Deep, deep eternity!" (From "Zarathustra's Roundelay")

50

This Countenance has been decisively rejected by the whole of contemporary culture. Given externally in the whole development of Europe's ecclesial life, It has not been imprinted in the most inner human impulse. This impulse, flowing namelessly and breaking through into the consciousness of its individual bearers, has violently rejected all the imprints of the ecclesial countenance: first in the vision of Paul who did not see Christ, and then in the person of Augustine it discarded all the psycho-spiritual representations of the countenance of the 4th and 5th centuries, tracing its unexpected channels in the formerly hidden *supra-spiritual* region. The power of thought poured therein: all the countenances, images, icons, and cults were destroyed by the flow of modern philosophy, streaming its grotesque music from the channel of religious forms. But this philosophy, too, was squeezed into the fixed "frame" of sterile rationalism, which dominated the 18th and 19th centuries. Nietzsche rejected all the "frames" as well as all the "icons"; he did not accept the flesh that sacrificed to idols, throwing himself instead into the purest rhythms of his nameless hopes; and with the thundering sun flaming from the center of his soul, he showed us a shimmering glimmer of the new culture.

The second Zarathustra is its herald, the herald of the second sun, the sun of the heart. The *second Zarathustra's* solar words radiate a limpid brightness, though his sun is a midnight sun. He can say about himself:

> Sundered within myself
> As if with the murk of non-being,
> Crucified within myself,
> I glow with the light of "I."
> In this waste land of the dark world
> My arm grows:
> Into the solarless spaces
> "I" solarly stretches.[62]

62. Variant of lines from Bely's poem "I" (1917).

He found out about "I"—the second Sun; the second coming of "I" (in our "I") he proclaimed as the coming into our "I" of the Midnight sun. But in formulating this knowledge as the doctrine of the superman, he erred: he didn't understand that he was awaiting "Man" in himself—ahead of himself, in the flight of instants of the times to come. As for his time, it was a circle; one standing at the apex rotates in the circle and *always returns.*

He didn't realize that the wheel of the flight of instants is within man; this wheel consists only of the spaces between the spokes of the intelligent wheel of the heart; and standing at the point of "I" within "I" is the brightened countenance of the circle of the Sun; and this countenance (whatever one calls it—man, superman, or God) is "I." It is the "I" of the whole world and the "I" of man; and the manifested union of the two "I's" is Christ.

Zarathustra is a presentiment of the rising Sun, but this sun is the bud of the unopened Rose, of Christ or "I." Time runs in a circle; in time all the Zarathustras (the second as well as the first) are heralds. That is what Zarathustra's rays sang us—with the coming of light.

The second coming—is real!

The disclosure of the glimmering mystery will be the task of culture. All the strata that enchain culture will be uncovered; it was formed by the premature materialization of the life-giving impulse; the life-impulse of Paul's "vision" was materialized in church dogmatics, in relation to which Augustine is, of course, a Protestant. Augustine was materialized in proportion to the dematerialization of scholastic thought, whose crystals were deposited as the dense stone of the cathedrals. Meanwhile, life-impulses flowed from the cathedrals in Bach's gurgling streams; Bach himself was materialized in the developed musical canons, and the life-impulses, seeping from art into the heart's blood, boiled up as the "revolt" against all. "Revolt" itself was materialized: the circular motion of Nietzsche's time erupted out of the pedestal of revolt, out of the statue of Superman-Antichrist, and it erupted with the most ineffable and nameless tenderness—with the Impulse of the Heart.

The new name (the "revolt" of revolt, the "I" of "I" itself) is Christ.

So finde im Niedergang
Und in des Todes Nacht

Der Schöpfung neuen Anfang,
Des Morgens junge Macht.[63]

51

The dogmas of our culture have been reincarnated in humanity, folding up spirally into a single point, and this point is "I." "I"—the free "I"—is the apex of an enormous cone: from its base (a circle) to the apex (a shining point) ran a spiral. If the circle is the zodiac that encircled 1st century humanity, then the point is "I" (man who lives today, in the 20th century). If the cone of time is turned, then the line (or spiral) in this new cross section disappears; we see *a circle with a point in the middle*. The point is "I" situated in 1915 in old Basel; the circle represents the dogmas of the 1st century; and the catastrophe of culture consists in a natural displacement of vision perpendicularly toward history. It seems that the spiral running (in the course of twenty centuries) from the enormous circle to the small point, to "I," is completed at that moment: the circle of the coming (the dogma) and "I" (the one who has come) are mysteriously connected; the mystery of the coming is the mystery of the coming of "I" (completely freely)—into Basel.

If a man sought to outlive himself as one who has come and if he viewed the whole history of more than nineteen centuries as the removal of the seals revealing the mission of (my) "I" which is experiencing here, in Basel, the global Golgotha—then to him has been revealed all that which from out of depths of Nietzsche's consciousness produced the craziest of cries: "Ecce homo," the consequence of which was the last signature of the crazy Nietzsche, announcing that he is the Crucified One (Dionysus).

But at that instant the opposite is also revealed: "I," ripped apart and crucified in itself, observes an enormous night within itself: The Sun is shining within "I," but the Sun Itself—the Circle of the Sun—is the Countenance rising in me: "I," rising in "I," is separated from "I" by an unending distance ("I is the path and aspiration toward the dis-

63. "Thus in descent and in the dead of night find the creation of a new beginning and the young power of the morning." (From Rudolf Steiner's Christmas lecture, Berlin, December 17, 1906)

tant"). The distant approaches the terrifying labor of the overcoming of Consciousness; I bear the whole Sun within myself but "I" am not the Sun, and if I were to express graphically the relation of the "point" (the personal "I") to the Sun within me, I would have to draw far from the apex of the history of the twenty centuries (the cone)—a circle, and then draw a line to it. I would get an inverted cone: the "point," instant, or "I" living in Basel would understand that only in the future can "I" truly become the sun that Nietzsche saw for the first time as an opening into possibility. The following moment after Nietzsche is a displacement of the perspective of consciousness that is perpendicular to Nietzsche's view of "I" but opposite to the view of history: the sun is approaching and will become the surface of life—perhaps after twenty centuries.

The second coming—the transubstantiation in Christ of the whole planet and of "I" dwelling in Basel, in Petersburg, in Saratov—will truly take place.

This knowledge is now *the mathematics of the new soul; the mathematics of this spiritual science* is a portent of the culture to come.

We now stand at the point of intersection of the cones—in Nietzsche; through his revolt, through his negations, through knowledge of the mystery of the free, stellar "I," all shall pass as through the eye of the needle that has now cut history in two: We hear the cries of Kierkegaard's "unhappiest of men" on one side and of Max Stirner's "Unique One" on the other; in the center we see "the crucified Dionysus" (the esoteric name Nietzsche gave himself).

52

I took flowers to the grave of the reposing Friedrich Nietzsche. That was near Leipzig. I remember: I fell on the gravestone, kissed it, and felt vividly that suddenly the cone of history had mysteriously fallen away from me. I felt vividly that the event of our journey to the remains of the reposing Nietzsche was an event of immense cosmic significance and that I, kneeling at his grave, was at the apex of a monstrous historical tower which had collapsed under me, plunging me into emptiness; and I said: "Ecce homo."

And I *am* "Ecce homo."

That's what I felt. And I also felt that an improbable Sun was flying down—into me!

The experiences at Nietzsche's grave produced a strange illness in me, which continued in Basel: It often seemed to me that I was crucified, and in that condition I roamed above the green, rapidly flowing currents of the Rhine. Thorns pierced *the brow of the epoch* which I bore above the Rhine; it seemed to me that I bore the death of culture within myself. It was strange: the thorns of my life were revealed to me in Dornach.[64]

The raven cried spitefully at me there.

Here—in Basel and Dornach—I gaze for a long time at the orange-red tiles of the houses and am surrounded, as was Nietzsche, by cretins. It is here that Morgenstern was cremated. From here I can hear the chatter of the cannons in Alsace, and it is here that I experience the death of culture. And it is here that I greet the birth of a new culture and contemplate the two domes of the bright building.[65]

64. The center of Anthroposophy.
65. Steiner's Johannes Building.